Great Taste ~ Low Fat

MAIN-DISH SALADS

TIME
LIFE
BOOKS

ALEXANDRIA, VIRGINIA

TABLE OF CONTENTS

Shrimp Caesar Salad

~

page 114

Chicken & Turkey

Beef, Pork & Lamb

Vegetables

Texas Barbecued Beef Salad

page 127

Fish & Shellfish

On the Grill

INTRODUCTION

Many people think of salad as an appetizer, accompaniment, or the fussy featured dish at a "ladies' lunch," and not as the main course of a serious meal. But salads can be so much more than a leaf of lettuce and a dab of dressing: Warm potatoes with grilled shrimp, for example; or noodles, sea-fresh scallops, and water chestnuts; or strips of broiled lamb with asparagus; or sweet potatoes and ham accented with tart watercress. Meat, poultry, and fish play the same role in these salads as they do in a well-balanced diet: They're used in proportions that keep the overall fat content low.

SALADS IN THEIR SEASONS

Sandy Gluck, who creates our recipes, is a city-dweller who dreams of someday tending a garden outside her kitchen door. There, she could watch tomatoes and eggplants ripen on the vine; pluck peas and snap beans at their tender peak; dig marble-sized new potatoes; and gather dewy basil leaves. But Sandy does have plenty of produce to choose from at the huge farmers' market found in her neighborhood four days a week. "The farmers' market is an inspiration as well as a place to shop. It reminds me of what's in season so I don't get into the rut of cooking the same vegetables all year round."

Even if you do your produce shopping at a supermarket, it's wise to consider the season when making salads. Most of us are fortunate to have access to a variety of vegetables and fruits throughout the year, but enjoying foods in their seasons is a pleasure that connects us with nature's cycles. So use tomatoes when you can get full-flavored beauties, enjoy asparagus and melons when they're being harvested in your part of the country, and buy corn or sugar snap peas when you can get them within a day of picking. This doesn't mean that salads must disappear at the end of the season: Root vegetables like potatoes, carrots, turnips, and parsnips are available in the fall and winter; and pasta, bean, and grain salads are most welcome in cool weather, too.

TAKE YOUR PICK

There's a salad to suit every taste and every occasion, and our recipes put them all within reach by using familiar, readily available ingredients. Naturally, we combine these everyday seasonings and condiments in ways that yield distinctive and ultra-flavorful results. Our Chicken & Turkey chapter makes brilliant use of ever-popular poultry in such recipes as Chicken Taco Salad, Sesame Chicken Salad with Ginger Dressing, and Turkey-Pasta Salad with Pesto Dressing. The Beef, Pork &

Lamb chapter offers creative dishes including an innovative Summer Pork Salad with Melon, Rice Salad with Lamb and Apples, and a Florentine Beef Salad worthy of a fine Tuscan restaurant. The Vegetables chapter departs from the expected with recipes like Fresh Corn Confetti Salad with Jack Cheese, Mushroom Barley Salad, and Hoppin' John Salad (based on a classic Southern rice dish). In addition to two tuna salads—one made with fresh tuna, one with canned—the Fish & Shellfish chapter features an updated Crab Louis, Spicy Italian Shrimp Salad, Seafood Salad with Lemon-Pepper Dressing, and much more. The combination of barbecued foods and crisp greens has real appeal, and some of our most unexpected salads get their start On the Grill: Cajun Chicken Salad, Texas Barbecued Beef Salad, and Margarita Scallop Salad are just three tempting examples.

"Secrets of Low-Fat Salads" explains how we reduce the fat in different kinds of dressings and offers advice on salad greens. There's also a page of tips on preparing many of the vegetables used in this book. But don't worry about having to perfect any special techniques before you start serving mouth-watering main-dish salads: Deliciously fresh ingredients and this exceptional recipe collection are all you really need.

CONTRIBUTING EDITORS

***Sandra Rose Gluck**, a New York City chef, has years of experience creating delicious low-fat recipes that are quick to prepare. Her secret for satisfying results is to always aim for great taste and variety. By combining readily available, fresh ingredients with simple cooking techniques, Sandra has created the perfect recipes for today's busy lifestyles.*

***Grace Young** has been the director of a major test kitchen specializing in low-fat and health-related cookbooks for over 12 years. Grace oversees the development, taste testing, and nutritional analysis of every recipe in Great Taste-Low Fat. Her goal is simple: take the work and worry out of low-fat cooking so that you can enjoy delicious, healthy meals every day.*

***Kate Slate** has been a food editor for almost 20 years, and has published thousands of recipes in cookbooks and magazines. As the Editorial Director of Great Taste-Low Fat, Kate combined simple, easy to follow directions with practical low-fat cooking tips. The result is guaranteed to make your low-fat cooking as rewarding and fun as it is foolproof.*

NUTRITION

Every recipe in *Great Taste-Low Fat* provides per-serving values for the nutrients listed in the chart at right. The daily intakes listed in the chart are based on those recommended by the USDA and presume a nonsedentary lifestyle. The nutritional emphasis in this book is not only on controlling calories, but on reducing total fat grams. Research has shown that dietary fat metabolizes more easily into body fat than do carbohydrates and protein. In order to control the amount of fat in a given recipe and in your diet in general, no more than 30 percent of the calories should come from fat.

Nutrient	Women	Men
Fat	<65 g	<80 g
Calories	2000	2500
Saturated fat	<20 g	<25 g
Carbohydrate	300 g	375 g
Protein	50 g	65 g
Cholesterol	<300 mg	<300 mg
Sodium	<2400 mg	<2400 mg

These recommended daily intakes are averages used by the Food and Drug Administration and are consistent with the labeling on all food products. Although the values for cholesterol and sodium are the same for all adults, the other intake values vary depending on gender, ideal weight, and activity level. Check with a physician or nutritionist for your own daily intake values.

SECRETS OF LOW-FAT SALADS

MAIN-DISH SALADS

Making salads that are low in fat doesn't seem like much of a trick: After all, how much fat could there be in a bowl of vegetables? But when you pour on a rich dressing, you end up with a dish in which a high percentage of the calories come from fat. We've reversed those proportions by making our salads heartier and slimming down our dressings. Make no mistake, these are substantial, filling main dishes. Many of the salads contain lean meat, poultry, or fish, while the meatless salads get their protein from legumes (such as beans or lentils) or grains (such as rice and barley). You might want to serve some bread or rolls alongside, but other than that, these salads need no accompaniments.

DESIGN THE DRESSING

Our effort to reduce the fat in our dressings meant rethinking the basics. For instance, a classic vinaigrette (oil and vinegar) dressing calls for an oil-to-vinegar ratio of three to one. Our vinaigrettes require less oil because we use milder vinegars (rice vinegar, for instance) and often substitute broth or juice for some of the oil. Mayonnaise-based dressings, such as Green Goddess or Thousand Island, also present problems, because mayonnaise itself is high in fat. But our

thick, creamy dressings take shape around more healthful ingredients such as: reduced-fat mayonnaise, part-skim ricotta, low-fat cottage cheese, buttermilk, reduced-fat cream cheese, light sour cream, and low-fat yogurt. Mashed or puréed vegetables, such as potatoes or roasted bell peppers, give some dressings full-bodied texture, while others are thickened and flavored with ingredients like honey, mustard, chutney, or chili sauce. Cooked dressings are, like sauces, thickened with flour or cornstarch. In any case, we've made the dressings so flavorful—through the use of herbs, spices, fat-free condiments, and other potent seasonings—that you'll never miss the fat.

DOUBLE THE FLAVOR

In recipes made with roasted, grilled, or sautéed meat or poultry, we like to reinforce the flavor by making double use of seasoning mixtures (herbs, spices, salt, pepper, etc.). Often part of a mixture is rubbed onto meat or poultry, while the rest goes into a dressing. For the same reason, we sometimes use the savory pan juices (or poaching liquid) from cooked meat or poultry in dressings.

In any recipe where the pan juices or broth are *not* used, you can—if it's more convenient—substitute leftover (or store-bought, ready-to-eat) meat or poultry for what is prepared in the recipe.

As a general rule, if a recipe calls for 12 ounces of uncooked meat or poultry, you will need 9 ounces of cooked as a substitute.

MIX UP THE GREENS

Don't limit yourself to just a few types of greens when there's such a tempting variety to choose from: tender lettuces such as Bibb, Boston, and buttercrunch; soft yet sturdy red leaf and green leaf; crisp, unwilting iceberg and Romaine; and assertive greens, including arugula, watercress, radicchio, endive (Belgian and curly), and escarole, whose leaves are a bit tart or peppery. Don't forget the full "green" flavor of spinach, and the refreshing crunchiness of red and green cabbage. You can make a salad with just one type of green, but a mixture can be much more appealing. Mix and match for lively color and texture.

Mesclun (a Provençal word meaning "mixture") is a medley of colorful salad greens. It includes a variety of leaves from young lettuces, such as red and green leaf, red and green Romaine, and frisée (narrow-leaved curly endive), along with tender baby leaves of assertively flavored greens like mustard, chard, and arugula. It may also contain fresh herbs—basil or mint, perhaps—and edible flowers, often nasturtiums, which have a peppery bite.

Iceberg lettuce

Red cabbage

Spinach

Green leaf lettuce

Red leaf lettuce

Green cabbage

Romaine lettuce

Chicory

Escarole

Mesclun

Boston lettuce

Endive

Radicchio

Bibb lettuce

Watercress

Arugula

VEGETABLE PREPARATION

What happens to vegetables between the grocery bag and the salad bowl? A bit of washing, peeling, trimming, and cutting. Here's how to do it:

ASPARAGUS. Cut or snap off bottoms if tough (when bent, stalks should break where tough portion begins). Cut stalks into short lengths.

AVOCADOS. Halve by slicing around "equator"; twist halves to separate. Thrust knife edge into pit, then twist to remove pit. Slip off skin, or scoop out flesh with a serving spoon.

BELL PEPPERS. Cut crosswise to remove top like a cap, then halve pepper lengthwise. With your fingers, pull out the spongy ribs and attached seeds.

BROCCOLI. Cut about 1 inch below buds to create florets; if recipe does not use stems, save for another day (use as a side dish or in a soup).

CABBAGE. Quarter through stem; cut out and discard core. To shred, place on a cutting board and, using a large chef's knife, slice lengthwise.

CARROTS. To julienne, halve crosswise, then halve each piece lengthwise. Lay pieces flat and cut into thin slices. Stack slices and cut into thin sticks. To shred, use the coarse side of a grater or shred carrots in a food processor.

CAULIFLOWER. Peel off leaves; trim thick base from stems. Cut about 1 inch below buds to create florets; if stems are not needed, save for another use.

CUCUMBERS. Peel cucumbers with a vegetable peeler after trimming both ends. To seed, halve cucumbers lengthwise and scoop out seeds with a teaspoon or melon baller.

EGGPLANT. Cut thin slices from both top and bottom, then peel with a vegetable peeler.

FENNEL. Cut off stalks and trim base of the bulb. Holding a large knife perpendicular to base, cut into thin slices.

GARLIC. Gently flatten clove under blade of a heavy knife to loosen skin, then peel. To mince, sliver clove lengthwise, then chop crosswise.

GREENS. Wash greens quickly but thoroughly in cool water, then spin or shake dry; wrap in a kitchen towel to blot remaining moisture. Tear (don't cut) leafy greens into bite-size pieces.

HERBS. Rinse under cool water; shake dry. Chop leaves with a chef's knife or snip with scissors.

MUSHROOMS. Rinse briefly and pat dry or wipe clean with a damp towel; trim stems. Slice button mushrooms vertically. Cut tough stems from shiitake mushrooms (save to use in broth or soup) and slice the caps.

ONIONS. Cut off top and bottom, then peel off skin. Halve crosswise and chop or dice; or cut crosswise into thick or thin slices.

PEAS. Cut or snip off both ends of snow-pea pods. Pinch off the tips of sugar snaps and pull off strings from both sides of the pod.

SCALLIONS. Trim base and tips and pull away any wilted leaves; to julienne, cut into short lengths, then lengthwise into strips.

SHALLOTS. Peel shallots as you would onions; chop them as you would mince garlic.

TOMATOES. To core whole tomatoes, use a paring knife to cut a cone-shaped plug from the stem end. If tomatoes are very watery, halve them and squeeze out excess liquid before using in salads.

CHICKEN & TURKEY

1

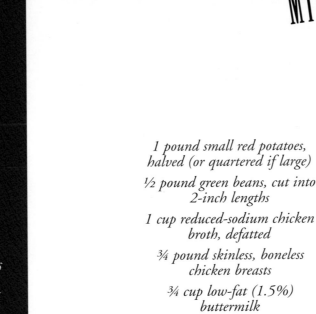

MINTED CHICKEN SALAD

SERVES: 4
WORKING TIME: 20 MINUTES
TOTAL TIME: 30 MINUTES

There are some lively Greek accents in this lightly dressed salad. The tangy lemon dressing is enlivened with a burst of fresh mint, and the salad is topped with Greek feta cheese. The contrast between the salty cheese and the refreshing mint is a real palate-pleaser. To round out the meal, all you need to serve is a crusty loaf of peasant bread.

1 pound small red potatoes, halved (or quartered if large)

½ pound green beans, cut into 2-inch lengths

1 cup reduced-sodium chicken broth, defatted

¾ pound skinless, boneless chicken breasts

¾ cup low-fat (1.5%) buttermilk

2 tablespoons fresh lemon juice

1 tablespoon honey

¼ teaspoon salt

¼ teaspoon cayenne pepper

⅓ cup chopped fresh mint

8 cups packed fresh spinach leaves (about 12 ounces)

2 cups cherry tomatoes, halved

1 cup crumbled feta cheese (3 ounces)

1. In a medium pot of boiling water, cook the potatoes until firm-tender, about 10 minutes. Add the green beans for the last 2 minutes of cooking time. Drain well.

2. Meanwhile, in a medium skillet, bring the broth to a boil over medium heat. Reduce to a simmer, add the chicken, and cook, turning once, until the chicken is cooked through, about 10 minutes. With a slotted spoon, transfer the chicken to a plate. (Reserve the broth for another use.) When cool enough to handle, cut the chicken on the diagonal into ½-inch slices.

3. In a large bowl, whisk together the buttermilk, lemon juice, honey, salt, and cayenne. Add the mint and whisk again. Add the potatoes and green beans, chicken, spinach, and tomatoes, tossing to combine. Divide among 4 plates, top with the feta, and serve warm, at room temperature, or chilled.

Helpful hints: You can make the salad up to 8 hours in advance; do not sprinkle the feta over until just before serving. If you're watching your sodium intake, rinse the feta under cool water and drain it well before crumbling it. This will wash away some of the brine the cheese is packed in.

FAT: 8G/20%
CALORIES: 362
SATURATED FAT: 4.1G
CARBOHYDRATE: 43G
PROTEIN: 35G
CHOLESTEROL: 71MG
SODIUM: 680MG

Turkey-Pasta Salad with Pesto Dressing

SERVES: 4
WORKING TIME: 30 MINUTES
TOTAL TIME: 35 MINUTES

W*hat*
a terrific buffet
centerpiece this salad
would make (and you
can easily double the
recipe if necessary).
The pesto dressing
boasts a full, true basil
flavor, but is much
lower in fat than a
traditional pesto.
The secret lies in
replacing much of the
oil with chicken
broth—a trick that
works with many types
of salad dressing.

4 cloves garlic, peeled
8 ounces ziti pasta
3 cups broccoli florets
4 teaspoons olive oil
¾ pound turkey cutlets, cut into
2 x ½-inch strips
¾ cup reduced-sodium chicken
broth, defatted
1½ cups packed fresh basil leaves
½ teaspoon salt
⅓ cup grated Parmesan cheese
1 red bell pepper, cut into
½-inch-wide strips
1 yellow bell pepper, cut into
½-inch-wide strips

1. In a large pot of boiling water, cook the garlic for 2 minutes to blanch. With a slotted spoon, remove the garlic and set aside. Add the ziti to the boiling water and cook until just tender, adding the broccoli for the last 1 minute of cooking time. Drain well.

2. Meanwhile, in a large nonstick skillet, heat 2 teaspoons of the oil until hot but not smoking over medium heat. Add the turkey and cook, stirring frequently, until cooked through, about 4 minutes. With a slotted spoon, transfer the turkey to a plate. Add the broth to the skillet and bring to a boil, scraping up any browned bits that cling to the pan.

3. In a food processor, combine the broth from the skillet, the blanched garlic, basil, salt, and the remaining 2 teaspoons oil and process until smooth, about 1 minute. Transfer to a large bowl and whisk in the Parmesan until well combined. Add the pasta, broccoli, turkey, and bell peppers, stirring to coat. Serve at room temperature or chilled.

Helpful hints: As is true of many pasta salads, this dish actually benefits from being made up to 8 hours in advance. The extra time allows the pasta to absorb more of the dressing. You can use 2 red or yellow bell peppers instead of 1 of each, if you like.

very good!
Make again
'14'

FAT: 9G/18%
CALORIES: 456
SATURATED FAT: 2.2G
CARBOHYDRATE: 59G
PROTEIN: 37G
CHOLESTEROL: 58MG
SODIUM: 595MG

Rice salads, every bit as satisfying as potato or pasta salads, make terrific main courses. Along with chicken and colorful vegetables, this one features some exotic touches— coconut, chili sauce, lime juice, and the sunny, tropical taste of golden mango. If you can't get a mango, however, you can make this salad with peaches or nectarines instead.

CHICKEN-MANGO SALAD

SERVES: 4
WORKING TIME: 25 MINUTES
TOTAL TIME: 35 MINUTES

1 cup long-grain rice

3 cloves garlic, minced

½ teaspoon salt

3 tablespoons flaked coconut

*¾ pound skinless, boneless
chicken breasts*

½ teaspoon paprika

½ cup chili sauce

¼ cup fresh lime juice

2 tablespoons honey

1 tablespoon olive oil

*1 mango (12 ounces), peeled and
cut into ½-inch cubes (see tip)*

*1 cucumber, peeled, halved
lengthwise, seeded, and thinly
sliced*

*1 red onion, halved and thinly
sliced*

2 cups cherry tomatoes, halved

4 cups mixed torn greens

1. Preheat the broiler. In a medium saucepan, bring 2¼ cups of water to a boil. Add the rice, garlic, and ¼ teaspoon of the salt, reduce to a simmer, cover, and cook until the rice is tender, about 17 minutes. Stir in the coconut. Transfer the rice to a large bowl, fluff with a fork, and set aside to cool to room temperature.

2. Meanwhile, rub the chicken with the paprika and the remaining ¼ teaspoon salt. Broil 6 inches from the heat for 4 minutes per side, or until cooked through. When cool enough to handle, slice the chicken crosswise into ½-inch pieces.

3. In a large bowl, combine the chili sauce, lime juice, honey, and oil. Add the mango, cucumber, onion, and tomatoes, stirring to combine. Add the rice, chicken, and greens, tossing to combine. Divide among 4 plates and serve warm, at room temperature, or chilled.

Helpful hint: The salad can be made up to 8 hours in advance; do not add the greens until just before serving.

FAT: 7G/14%
CALORIES: 468
SATURATED FAT: 1.9G
CARBOHYDRATE: 78G
PROTEIN: 27G
CHOLESTEROL: 49MG
SODIUM: 816MG

TIP

Score each mango half into squares, cutting to, but not through, the skin. Turn the half inside out to pop the cut pieces outward. Cut the pieces away from the skin.

Fried Chicken Salad

SERVES: 4
WORKING TIME: 35 MINUTES
TOTAL TIME: 35 MINUTES

1 pound small red potatoes, halved (or quartered if large)

1½ cups frozen corn kernels

2 tablespoons white wine or distilled white vinegar

2 tablespoons flour

¾ teaspoon salt

¼ teaspoon freshly ground black pepper

¾ pound skinless, boneless chicken breasts

2 teaspoons olive oil

¼ cup reduced-sodium chicken broth, defatted

¾ cup low-fat (1.5%) buttermilk

2 tablespoons reduced-fat mayonnaise

1 red bell pepper, cut into ½-inch-wide strips

2 ribs celery, halved lengthwise and cut into 2-inch lengths

4 cups mixed torn greens

1. In a medium pot of boiling water, cook the potatoes until firm-tender, about 10 minutes. Add the corn for the last 1 minute of cooking time and drain well. Transfer to a large bowl and sprinkle with the vinegar.

2. Meanwhile, on a sheet of waxed paper, combine the flour, ¼ teaspoon of the salt, and the black pepper. Dredge the chicken in the flour mixture, shaking off the excess. In a medium nonstick skillet, heat the oil until hot but not smoking over medium heat. Add the chicken and cook, turning it as it browns, until cooked through, about 4 minutes per side. Transfer the chicken to a plate and set aside. When cool enough to handle, thinly slice the chicken.

3. Add the broth to the skillet and cook for about 2 minutes, scraping up any browned bits that cling to the pan. Scrape the broth from the skillet into the bowl with the potatoes and corn. Add the buttermilk, mayonnaise, and the remaining ½ teaspoon salt, stirring until well combined. Add the chicken, bell pepper, celery, and greens, tossing to coat. Divide evenly among 4 plates and serve warm, at room temperature, or chilled.

Helpful hint: The salad can be made up to 12 hours in advance; do not add the greens until just before serving.

FAT: 7G/18%
CALORIES: 342
SATURATED FAT: 1.4G
CARBOHYDRATE: 45G
PROTEIN: 27G
CHOLESTEROL: 52MG
SODIUM: 622MG

Fried chicken, potato salad, and corn add up to good eating, American-country style. We've assembled these three components into a bountiful salad with down-home flavor. To keep the meal healthful, the skinless chicken is fried in very little oil and the dressing is based on a blend of low-fat buttermilk and reduced-fat mayonnaise.

CALIFORNIA CHICKEN SALAD WITH AVOCADO

SERVES: 4
WORKING TIME: 20 MINUTES
TOTAL TIME: 30 MINUTES

The state of California is the birthplace of many of America's favorite salads—which makes sense, because the Golden State supplies the nation with massive quantities of salad ingredients. This salad features avocado—an important California crop—as well as poached chicken breasts, red potatoes, tomatoes, and watercress.

1¼ pounds small red potatoes, quartered

1 cup reduced-sodium chicken broth, defatted

¼ teaspoon dried rosemary, crumbled

10 ounces skinless, boneless chicken breasts

2 bunches of watercress, tough stems removed

4 tomatoes

¼ cup fresh lime juice

1 tablespoon olive oil, preferably extra-virgin

½ teaspoon salt

⅓ cup diced avocado

1. In a medium pot of boiling water, cook the potatoes until firm-tender, about 10 minutes. Drain well.

2. Meanwhile, in a large skillet, bring the broth and rosemary to a boil over medium heat. Reduce to a simmer, add the chicken, cover, and cook, turning once, until the chicken is cooked through, about 10 minutes. Remove the chicken from the skillet and set aside. (Reserve the broth for another use.) When cool enough to handle, cut the chicken on the diagonal into ½-inch slices.

3. In a large bowl, toss together the potatoes and watercress. Cut 2 of the tomatoes into 6 wedges each and add to the bowl. In a small bowl, combine the lime juice, oil, and salt. Finely chop the 2 remaining tomatoes and add to the lime mixture. Pour all but ¼ cup of the tomato dressing over the mixture in the bowl, add the chicken, and toss to combine. Place on a large platter, drizzle with the reserved tomato dressing, sprinkle the avocado over, and serve warm, at room temperature, or chilled.

Helpful hint: You could replace half the watercress with a tender lettuce such as Bibb, and half with sprouts—preferably spicy ones like radish sprouts; alfalfa, bean, or lentil sprouts could be used as well.

FAT: 7G/22%
CALORIES: 283
SATURATED FAT: 1.1G
CARBOHYDRATE: 35G
PROTEIN: 23G
CHOLESTEROL: 41MG
SODIUM: 413MG

Turkey-Potato Salad

SERVES: 4
WORKING TIME: 35 MINUTES
TOTAL TIME: 40 MINUTES

*I*nstead of minced turkey awash in mayonnaise, enjoy this chunky mix of turkey, vegetables, and egg in a light but creamy dressing.

1 pound small red potatoes, quartered

1 tablespoon olive oil

¾ pound turkey cutlets

¾ teaspoon salt

½ cup reduced-sodium chicken broth, defatted

¾ cup plain nonfat yogurt

2 tablespoons reduced-fat sour cream

3 scallions, thinly sliced

1 zucchini, halved lengthwise and thinly sliced

2 cups halved cherry tomatoes

1 hard-cooked egg, cut into 8 wedges

1. In a medium pot of boiling water, cook the potatoes until firm-tender, about 10 minutes. Drain well.

2. Meanwhile, in a large nonstick skillet, heat the oil until hot but not smoking over medium heat. Sprinkle the turkey with G teaspoon of the salt and cook until cooked through, about 1 minute per side. Transfer the turkey to a plate.

3. Add the broth to the skillet and boil until reduced by half, about 3 minutes. Pour the reduced cooking liquid into a large bowl and whisk in the yogurt, sour cream, the remaining H teaspoon salt, and the scallions. Add the potatoes, zucchini, and tomatoes, tossing to combine. Cut the turkey into H-inch-wide strips and toss with the vegetable mixture. Divide among 4 plates, top each with 2 egg wedges, and serve warm, at room temperature, or chilled.

Helpful hints: You can make this salad up to 12 hours in advance; don't add the egg until just before serving, or the yolk may darken. For a perfect hard-cooked egg, place the egg in a saucepan, add cold water to cover by 1 inch, and bring to a boil over medium-high heat. As soon as the water comes to a boil, cover the pan, remove from the heat, and let stand for exactly 17 minutes. Peel the egg under cold running water.

FAT: 7G/21%
CALORIES: 294
SATURATED FAT: 1.6G
CARBOHYDRATE: 29G
PROTEIN: 29G
CHOLESTEROL: 109MG
SODIUM: 592MG

Asian Shredded Chicken Salad

SERVES: 4
WORKING TIME: 20 MINUTES
TOTAL TIME: 30 MINUTES

1½ cups reduced-sodium chicken broth, defatted

1 tablespoon reduced-sodium soy sauce

3 cloves garlic, minced

1 teaspoon ground ginger

¾ pound skinless, boneless chicken breasts

1 pound sweet potatoes, peeled and cut into 2 x ½-inch julienne strips

¼ pound snow peas, trimmed

2 tablespoons rice vinegar

1 tablespoon dark Oriental sesame oil

1 tablespoon honey

½ teaspoon salt

3 cups shredded red and green cabbage

1. In a medium skillet, combine the broth, soy sauce, garlic, and ginger and bring to a boil over medium heat. Reduce to a simmer, add the chicken, cover, and cook, turning once, until the chicken is cooked through, about 10 minutes. With a slotted spoon, transfer the chicken to a plate; reserve the cooking liquid. When cool enough to handle, shred the chicken with your fingers.

2. Bring the reserved cooking liquid to a boil over medium heat. Add the sweet potatoes, cover, and cook, stirring occasionally, until firm-tender, about 7 minutes. Add the snow peas and cook until the sweet potatoes are tender but not falling apart, about 2 minutes. Drain, reserving the cooking liquid.

3. In a large bowl, combine ¾ cup of the reserved cooking liquid, the vinegar, sesame oil, honey, and salt. Add the chicken, sweet potatoes, snow peas, and cabbage and toss until well combined. Divide among 4 plates and serve warm, at room temperature, or chilled.

Helpful hint: Napa cabbage is a crisp, pale-green Asian cabbage that forms an elongated head. You could substitute it for one or both types of the cabbage called for here.

FAT: 5G/17%
CALORIES: 265
SATURATED FAT: 0.8G
CARBOHYDRATE: 31G
PROTEIN: 24G
CHOLESTEROL: 49MG
SODIUM: 709MG

This substantial slaw is made with crunchy cabbage and snow peas, sweet potatoes, and slivers of chicken.

21

THAI CHICKEN AND PEANUT SALAD

SERVES: 4
WORKING TIME: 25 MINUTES
TOTAL TIME: 35 MINUTES

I t's nice to be able to fix an exotic-tasting Asian-style dinner without having to shop around for obscure ingredients. We've made some clever substitutions in this recipe that let you create true Thai taste using standard supermarket items. The dressing is made with fresh basil, plum jam, ketchup, lime juice, and that all-American staple, peanut butter.

1 cup reduced-sodium chicken broth, defatted

¾ pound skinless, boneless chicken breasts

⅓ cup chopped fresh basil or mint

2 tablespoons plum jam

2 tablespoons ketchup

2 tablespoons creamy peanut butter

2 tablespoons fresh lime juice

½ teaspoon hot pepper sauce

½ teaspoon salt

8 ounces fettuccine, broken into thirds

6 ounces green beans, halved crosswise

1 red bell pepper, cut into ¼-inch-wide strips

1 yellow bell pepper, cut into ¼-inch-wide strips

1 cucumber, peeled, halved lengthwise, seeded, and thinly sliced

1 tablespoon chopped peanuts

1. In a medium skillet, bring the broth to a boil. Reduce to a simmer, add the chicken, cover, and cook until the chicken is cooked through, about 10 minutes. With a slotted spoon, transfer the chicken to a plate; reserve the cooking liquid. When cool enough to handle, shred the chicken with your fingers.

2. In a large bowl, combine ¼ cup of the reserved cooking liquid, the basil, plum jam, ketchup, peanut butter, lime juice, hot pepper sauce, and salt.

3. Meanwhile, in a large pot of boiling water, cook the pasta and green beans until the pasta is just tender. Add the bell peppers for the last 1 minute of cooking time. Drain well.

4. Add the chicken, pasta, green beans, bell peppers, and cucumber to the bowl with the basil mixture, tossing well to combine. Divide the salad among 4 plates, sprinkle the peanuts over, and serve warm, at room temperature, or chilled.

Helpful hints: You can prepare the salad up to 8 hours in advance; do not sprinkle the peanuts over until just before serving. You can use 2 red or yellow bell peppers instead of 1 of each, if you like.

FAT: 9G/18%
CALORIES: 441
SATURATED FAT: 1.6G
CARBOHYDRATE: 59G
PROTEIN: 33G
CHOLESTEROL: 103MG
SODIUM: 565MG

CHICKEN NOODLE SALAD

SERVES: 4
WORKING TIME: 20 MINUTES
TOTAL TIME: 30 MINUTES

You loved it as a soup, now try it as a salad! Not surprisingly, the combination of tender chicken and ribbony pasta works as well in a main-course salad as in does in a heart-warming soup. All the familiar touches are here: carrots, peas, fresh dill, and—as in the best homemade chicken soup—subtle hints of lemon and ginger.

8 ounces fettuccine

1½ cups reduced-sodium chicken broth, defatted

¼ teaspoon freshly ground black pepper

¼ teaspoon ground ginger

¾ pound skinless, boneless chicken breasts

2 carrots, halved lengthwise and thinly sliced

1 cup frozen peas

⅓ cup reduced-fat sour cream

2 tablespoons reduced-fat mayonnaise

½ teaspoon grated lemon zest

1 tablespoon fresh lemon juice

⅓ cup snipped fresh dill

½ teaspoon salt

2 ribs celery, halved lengthwise and thinly sliced

1. In a large pot of boiling water, cook the fettuccine until just tender. Drain well.

2. Meanwhile, in a large skillet, bring the broth, pepper, and ginger to a boil over medium heat. Reduce to a simmer, add the chicken, cover, and cook, turning once, until the chicken is cooked through, about 10 minutes. Add the carrots for the last 2 minutes of cooking time. Add the peas to the skillet and remove from the heat. Reserving the cooking liquid, drain the chicken and vegetables. When the chicken is cool enough to handle, cut it into ½-inch cubes.

3. In a large bowl, combine ½ cup of the reserved cooking liquid, the sour cream, mayonnaise, lemon zest, lemon juice, dill, and salt. Add the pasta, chicken, carrots, peas, and celery, tossing to combine. Serve at room temperature or chilled.

Helpful hint: You can cook the chicken and vegetables up to 12 hours in advance; refrigerate them in the broth rather than draining them right after cooking.

FAT: 8G/17%
CALORIES: 415
SATURATED FAT: 2.4G
CARBOHYDRATE: 54G
PROTEIN: 32G
CHOLESTEROL: 110MG
SODIUM: 554MG

Picnic
planners, take note:
This snappy-tasting
macaroni salad puts
the bland original in
the shade, and is no
mere side dish but a
meal in itself. The
macaroni is tossed with
turkey, corn, and
cubed tomato; the
robust dressing is made
with tomato-vegetable
juice and balsamic
vinegar. And once the
pasta's cooked, the
salad is a simple one-
bowl proposition.

Summer Turkey Salad

SERVES: 4
WORKING TIME: 15 MINUTES
TOTAL TIME: 25 MINUTES

4 ounces elbow macaroni

½ cup low-sodium tomato-vegetable juice

2 tablespoons balsamic vinegar

2 tablespoons olive oil, preferably extra-virgin

1 tablespoon no-salt-added tomato paste

½ teaspoon dried oregano

½ teaspoon salt

¼ teaspoon freshly ground black pepper

¾ pound cooked turkey breast (see tip), cut into 2 x ½-inch julienne strips

2 cups frozen corn kernels, thawed

1 tomato, cut into ½-inch cubes

4 scallions, thinly sliced

⅓ cup chopped fresh parsley

1. In a large pot of boiling water, cook the pasta until just tender. Drain well.

2. In a large bowl, whisk together the tomato-vegetable juice, vinegar, oil, tomato paste, oregano, salt, and pepper. Add the pasta, turkey, corn, tomato, scallions, and parsley, tossing well to combine. Serve at room temperature or chilled.

Helpful hint: Tomato-vegetable juice comes in big bottles, but it's also sold in six-packs of 6-ounce cans—a useful size for recipes. Tomato-vegetable juice is also a refreshing, low-calorie snack.

FAT: 9G/21%
CALORIES: 378
SATURATED FAT: 1.4G
CARBOHYDRATE: 44G
PROTEIN: 33G
CHOLESTEROL: 71MG
SODIUM: 354MG

TIP

You can buy cooked turkey breast for this recipe, or poach turkey cutlets yourself using the following method: Bring 2 cups of water or broth to a boil in a large skillet over medium heat. Reduce to a simmer, add 1 pound of turkey breast cutlets, and cook, turning once, until the turkey is cooked through, 3 to 4 minutes.

CHICKEN SALAD WITH CREAMY CURRY DRESSING

SERVES: 4
WORKING TIME: 30 MINUTES
TOTAL TIME: 40 MINUTES

1 cup long-grain rice

¾ teaspoon salt

1 cup reduced-sodium chicken broth, defatted

¾ pound skinless, boneless chicken breasts

3 cups cauliflower florets

1½ cups frozen peas

¾ cup low-fat (1.5%) buttermilk

2 tablespoons reduced-fat mayonnaise

2 teaspoons curry powder

½ teaspoon ground cumin

½ teaspoon ground ginger

2 ribs celery, thinly sliced

1 red bell pepper, cut into ½-inch squares

2 cups seedless red and green grapes, halved

1. In a medium saucepan, bring 2¼ cups of water to a boil. Add the rice and ¼ teaspoon of the salt, reduce to a simmer, cover, and cook until the rice is tender, about 17 minutes. Transfer the rice to a large bowl and fluff with a fork.

2. Meanwhile, in a medium skillet, bring the broth to a boil over medium heat. Reduce to a simmer, add the chicken, cover, and cook, turning once, until the chicken is cooked through, about 10 minutes. With a slotted spoon, transfer the chicken to a plate; reserve the cooking liquid.

3. Return the cooking liquid to a boil, add the cauliflower, and cook until crisp-tender, about 4 minutes. Add the peas. Reserving the cooking liquid, drain the vegetables.

4. In a large bowl, combine the buttermilk, mayonnaise, curry powder, cumin, ginger, the remaining ½ teaspoon salt, and ⅓ cup of the reserved cooking liquid. Add the celery, bell pepper, grapes, cauliflower, and peas. Cut the chicken crosswise into ½-inch slices and add to the bowl, tossing to combine. Add the rice and toss again. Serve warm, at room temperature, or chilled.

Helpful hint: If you're serving the salad at room temperature and want to cool the rice quickly, spread it in a shallow pan and place it in the freezer for a few minutes before adding it to the salad.

FAT: 5G/10%
CALORIES: 443
SATURATED FAT: 1.2G
CARBOHYDRATE: 70G
PROTEIN: 31G
CHOLESTEROL: 52MG
SODIUM: 687MG

Since the sultry taste of curry goes beautifully with fruit, curried dishes are often served with mango chutney or raisin-studded rice. Here, jewel-like red and green grapes provide a sweet counterpoint to the lightly spicy dressing. Accompany the salad with warmed pita breads—white or whole wheat, plain or onion-flavored.

CHICKEN SALAD WITH TOMATO-CUCUMBER DRESSING

SERVES: 4
WORKING TIME: 25 MINUTES
TOTAL TIME: 25 MINUTES

The meaning of the term "chicken salad" has changed quite a bit in recent years. Nowadays it can describe a tempting platter of greens and grilled chicken breast as well as a mayonnaise-dressed sandwich filling. Here, thick slices of herbed chicken are served over a mix of colorful lettuces with a chunky "vegetable vinaigrette" that forms a substantial part of the dish.

¾ pound skinless, boneless chicken breasts

¾ teaspoon salt

¾ teaspoon dried oregano

1 tomato, coarsely chopped

2 kirby cucumbers or 1 regular cucumber, peeled, halved lengthwise, seeded, and cut into ¼-inch dice

1 red onion, cut into ¼-inch dice

2 tablespoons no-salt-added tomato paste

1 tablespoon olive oil, preferably extra-virgin

2 tablespoons red wine vinegar

½ teaspoon freshly ground black pepper

¼ teaspoon cayenne pepper

1 cup canned chick-peas, rinsed and drained

4 cups mesclun or mixed greens

1. Preheat the broiler. Sprinkle the chicken with ¼ teaspoon of the salt and ¼ teaspoon of the oregano. Broil 6 inches from the heat for 4 minutes per side, or until the chicken is cooked through. Transfer the chicken to a plate and when cool enough to handle, slice the chicken on the diagonal into ½-inch slices.

2. Meanwhile, in a large bowl, combine the tomato, cucumber, onion, tomato paste, oil, vinegar, black pepper, cayenne, the remaining ½ teaspoon salt, and remaining ½ teaspoon oregano. Toss well to combine. Add the chick-peas and toss again.

3. Place the greens on 4 plates. Top with the tomato mixture and chicken and serve warm, at room temperature, or chilled.

Helpful hints: Kirby cucumbers, sometimes called pickling cucumbers, are small and usually have fewer, smaller seeds than regular cucumbers. Choose firm, slender ones no more than 5 inches long.

FAT: 6G/24%
CALORIES: 221
SATURATED FAT: 0.9G
CARBOHYDRATE: 18G
PROTEIN: 25G
CHOLESTEROL: 49MG
SODIUM: 570MG

SESAME CHICKEN SALAD WITH GINGER DRESSING

SERVES: 4
WORKING TIME: 20 MINUTES
TOTAL TIME: 35 MINUTES

*T*he ever-popular Szechuan-style sesame noodles make a wonderful meal when combined with chicken, lettuce, and bell peppers.

8 ounces linguine

1 cup reduced-sodium chicken broth, defatted

2 cloves garlic, minced

¾ pound skinless, boneless chicken breasts

2 tablespoons dark Oriental sesame oil

2 tablespoons rice vinegar

1 tablespoon firmly packed dark or light brown sugar

1½ teaspoons ground ginger

½ teaspoon salt

3 scallions, halved lengthwise and cut into 2-inch lengths

1 red bell pepper, cut into 2 x ¼-inch strips

1 green bell pepper, cut into 2 x ¼-inch strips

6 cups shredded iceberg lettuce

1 tablespoon sesame seeds

1. In a large pot of boiling water, cook the linguine until just tender. Drain well.

2. Meanwhile, in a medium skillet, bring the broth and garlic to a boil over medium heat. Reduce to a simmer, add the chicken, cover, and cook, turning once, until the chicken is cooked through, about 10 minutes. With a slotted spoon, transfer the chicken to a plate. Return the cooking liquid to a boil and cook until reduced to ½ cup, about 3 minutes. Strain the liquid into a large bowl, discarding the solids.

3. Stir the sesame oil, vinegar, brown sugar, ginger, and salt into the bowl. Add the scallions, bell peppers, and linguine, tossing to combine. Cut the chicken lengthwise into ¼-inch-wide strips. Add to the bowl and toss well.

4. Place the lettuce in 4 bowls, top with the chicken mixture, sprinkle the sesame seeds over, and serve at room temperature or chilled.

Helpful hint: The salad may be prepared up to 8 hours ahead; arrange the salad over the lettuce and sprinkle with the sesame seeds just before serving.

FAT: 10G/21%
CALORIES: 428
SATURATED FAT: 1.6G
CARBOHYDRATE: 54G
PROTEIN: 30G
CHOLESTEROL: 49MG
SODIUM: 485MG

CHICKEN AND CHEDDAR SALAD

SERVES: 4
WORKING TIME: 20 MINUTES
TOTAL TIME: 35 MINUTES

1 cup apple cider or apple juice

2 tablespoons cider vinegar

3 cloves garlic, minced

½ teaspoon salt

½ teaspoon freshly ground
black pepper

10 ounces skinless, boneless
chicken breasts

1 tablespoon olive oil,
preferably extra-virgin

1 tablespoon honey

16-ounce can red kidney beans,
rinsed and drained

2 pears, halved, cored, and cut
into ¼-inch chunks

2 ribs celery, thinly sliced

4 cups mixed greens

½ cup shredded medium to
sharp Cheddar cheese
(2 ounces)

4 teaspoons coarsely chopped
walnuts

1. In a medium skillet, combine the cider, vinegar, garlic, salt, and pepper and bring to a boil over medium heat. Reduce to a simmer, add the chicken, cover, and cook, turning once, until the chicken is cooked through, about 10 minutes. With a slotted spoon, transfer the chicken to a plate. Return the cooking liquid to a boil over high heat and cook until reduced to ½ cup, about 3 minutes. Strain the liquid into a large bowl, discarding the solids.

2. Whisk the oil and honey into the reduced cooking liquid. Add the kidney beans, pears, and celery. Halve the chicken lengthwise, then cut it crosswise into ½-inch slices. Add the chicken to the bowl and toss to combine. Divide the greens among 4 plates. Spoon the chicken mixture over the greens, sprinkle with the Cheddar and walnuts, and serve warm, at room temperature, or chilled.

Helpful hint: You can make the chicken mixture up to 8 hours in advance; assemble the salad, greens, cheese, and walnuts just before serving.

FAT: 12G/29%
CALORIES: 375
SATURATED FAT: 3.9G
CARBOHYDRATE: 42G
PROTEIN: 28G
CHOLESTEROL: 56MG
SODIUM: 593MG

*T*he
*classic pairing of fruit
and cheese inspires this
salad made with pears,
Cheddar, and a
unique cider dressing.*

33

SICILIAN-STYLE CHICKEN SALAD

SERVES: 4
WORKING TIME: 20 MINUTES
TOTAL TIME: 30 MINUTES

The time-honored Italian marriage of pasta and tomatoes is the starting point for this multi-flavored salad. Wine vinegar, olive oil, and sage would be at home in Italian dishes from many regions, but the influence of sunny Sicily is clearly indicated through the inclusion of orange juice, fennel, raisins, and pine nuts. Accompany the salad with grissini (pencil-thin bread sticks).

8 ounces farfalle (bow-tie) pasta

¾ pound skinless, boneless chicken breasts

¾ teaspoon salt

½ teaspoon dried sage

½ teaspoon grated orange zest

¾ cup orange juice

3 tablespoons red wine vinegar

2 tablespoons no-salt-added tomato paste

2 tablespoons olive oil, preferably extra-virgin

½ teaspoon cayenne pepper

2 cups thinly sliced fennel or celery

1 cup coarsely chopped tomatoes

¼ cup golden or regular raisins

4 teaspoons pine nuts

1. In a large pot of boiling water, cook the pasta until just tender. Drain well.

2. Meanwhile, preheat the broiler. Sprinkle the chicken with ¼ teaspoon of the salt and the sage. Broil 6 inches from the heat for 4 minutes per side, or until cooked through.

3. In a large bowl, combine the orange zest, orange juice, vinegar, tomato paste, oil, cayenne, and the remaining ½ teaspoon salt. Add the fennel, tomatoes, raisins, and pasta, tossing well to combine. Slice the chicken crosswise on the diagonal into ½-inch slices. Add the chicken to the bowl and toss to combine.

4. Divide the chicken mixture among 4 plates, sprinkle with the pine nuts, and serve at room temperature or chilled.

Helpful hint: Fennel looks like the flattened base of a head of celery; the vegetable has a mild anise flavor. Look for a firm, unblemished fennel bulb; cut off the stalks and trim the root end before slicing it.

FAT: 11G/22%
CALORIES: 456
SATURATED FAT: 1.7G
CARBOHYDRATE: 61G
PROTEIN: 29G
CHOLESTEROL: 49MG
SODIUM: 534MG

The popular Italian appetizer of sliced tomatoes, mozzarella, and basil leaves drizzled with olive oil is properly known as "insalata caprese" (it's named for the island of Capri). We've rounded out this flavor-packed quartet of ingredients with chicken, pasta, and greens for a terrific main course. You can substitute another pasta for the small, tube-shaped ditalini.

Chicken Caprese

SERVES: 4
WORKING TIME: 15 MINUTES
TOTAL TIME: 25 MINUTES

5 ounces ditalini pasta or elbow macaroni (about 1¼ cups)
10 ounces skinless, boneless chicken breasts
¾ teaspoon salt
½ teaspoon dried oregano
2 cups cherry tomatoes, halved
½ cup chopped fresh basil
3 ounces part-skim mozzarella, cut into ½-inch cubes
2 tablespoons balsamic vinegar
1 tablespoon olive oil, preferably extra-virgin
4 cups mesclun or mixed greens

1. In a medium pot of boiling water, cook the pasta until just tender. Drain well.
2. Meanwhile, preheat the broiler. Rub the chicken with ¼ teaspoon of the salt and the oregano. Broil 6 inches from the heat for 4 minutes per side, or until just cooked through. Set the chicken aside and when cool enough to handle, cut it into 1-inch pieces.
3. In a large bowl, combine the tomatoes, basil, mozzarella, vinegar, oil, and the remaining ½ teaspoon salt. Add the chicken and pasta, tossing to combine. Place the greens on 4 plates, top with the chicken mixture, and serve at room temperature or chilled.

Helpful hint: For a more colorful salad, use half red cherry tomatoes and half yellow pear tomatoes.

FAT: 10G/29%
CALORIES: 316
SATURATED FAT: 3.6G
CARBOHYDRATE: 31G
PROTEIN: 26G
CHOLESTEROL: 58MG
SODIUM: 553MG

Even though it looks more like a grain than a pasta, couscous makes a great salad. The beadlike granules of pasta quickly absorb this well-seasoned dressing. Paprika, ginger, cumin, coriander, and cinnamon—all present here—are among the most important spices in the Moroccan kitchen and fresh cilantro is a favorite herb.

Moroccan Spiced Chicken Salad

Serves: 4
Working time: 20 minutes
Total time: 30 minutes

¾ pound skinless, boneless
chicken breasts

1 teaspoon paprika

¾ teaspoon salt

1 cup couscous (see tip)

2½ cups boiling water

¾ teaspoon ground ginger

½ teaspoon ground cumin

½ teaspoon ground coriander

¼ teaspoon cinnamon

3 carrots, halved lengthwise and
thinly sliced

2 green bell peppers, cut into
1-inch squares

1 tomato, finely chopped

4 teaspoons olive oil

1 tablespoon honey

¼ teaspoon freshly ground black
pepper

⅓ cup chopped fresh cilantro or
parsley

1. Preheat the broiler. Rub the chicken with ½ teaspoon of the paprika and ¼ teaspoon of the salt. Broil 6 inches from the heat for 4 minutes per side, or until cooked through. When cool enough to handle, cut into 1-inch chunks.

2. In a medium bowl, combine the couscous and boiling water. Stir well, cover, and let stand until the couscous has softened, about 5 minutes.

3. Meanwhile, in a large skillet, combine 2 cups of water, the ginger, cumin, coriander, and cinnamon. Bring to a boil over medium heat, add the carrots, and cook until crisp-tender, about 4 minutes. Add the bell peppers and cook until the peppers are crisp-tender, about 1 minute. With a slotted spoon, transfer the carrots and bell peppers to a large bowl; reserve the cooking liquid.

4. Add the tomato, oil, honey, black pepper, the remaining ½ teaspoon paprika, and remaining ½ teaspoon salt to the vegetables. Stir in ¼ cup of the reserved cooking liquid. Add the cilantro, couscous, and chicken, tossing to combine. Serve warm, at room temperature, or chilled.

Helpful hint: You can make the salad up to 8 hours in advance. If you do so, seed the tomato and squeeze out any excess liquid before chopping it. This way, the dressing will not become diluted.

Fat: 6g/15%
Calories: 368
Saturated Fat: 1g
Carbohydrate: 50g
Protein: 27g
Cholesterol: 49mg
Sodium: 497mg

TIP

Traditional North African couscous takes a long time and quite a bit of work to prepare. But the couscous found in supermarkets is precooked and requires only steeping. Fluff the softened couscous with a fork, which will separate the grains without crushing them.

SPANISH CHICKEN-RICE SALAD

SERVES: 4
WORKING TIME: 25 MINUTES
TOTAL TIME: 35 MINUTES

1 cup long-grain rice

¾ teaspoon salt

1 cup reduced-sodium chicken broth, defatted

2 cloves garlic, minced

¼ teaspoon freshly ground black pepper

⅛ teaspoon saffron, or ¼ teaspoon turmeric

¾ pound skinless, boneless chicken breasts

1 cup frozen peas

¼ cup fresh lemon juice

1 tablespoon olive oil, preferably extra-virgin

1 red bell pepper, cut into ½-inch squares

1 red onion, cut into ½-inch cubes

2 tablespoons slivered almonds

4 cups mixed torn greens

1. In a medium saucepan, bring 2¼ cups of water to a boil. Add the rice and ¼ teaspoon of the salt, reduce to a simmer, cover, and cook until the rice is tender, about 17 minutes. Transfer the rice to a large bowl and fluff with a fork.

2. Meanwhile, in a medium skillet, bring the broth, garlic, black pepper, and saffron to a boil over medium heat. Reduce to a simmer, add the chicken, cover, and cook, turning once, until the chicken is cooked through, about 10 minutes, adding the peas during the last 1 minute of cooking time. With a slotted spoon, transfer the chicken and peas to a plate. Strain the cooking liquid into a measuring cup and discard the solids. When the chicken is cool enough to handle, cut it into 1-inch cubes.

3. In a large bowl, combine 1 cup of the reserved cooking liquid, the lemon juice, oil, and the remaining ½ teaspoon salt. Add the rice, peas, chicken, bell pepper, onion, and almonds, tossing to combine. Divide the greens among 4 plates, spoon the salad over, and serve warm, at room temperature, or chilled.

Helpful hints: You can make the chicken-rice salad up to 12 hours in advance; don't spoon it over the greens until just before serving.

Here's a delicious version of arroz con pollo (chicken with rice) for you to enjoy: Not only have we translated the name into English, we've translated the saffron-tinted casserole into a cool, main-dish salad. This would be perfect for a summertime patio meal; bring out a basket of hot crusty rolls and offer a bowl of fresh fruit for dessert.

FAT: 7G/16%
CALORIES: 388
SATURATED FAT: 1.1G
CARBOHYDRATE: 52G
PROTEIN: 28G
CHOLESTEROL: 49MG
SODIUM: 663MG

BUFFALO CHICKEN SALAD

SERVES: 4
WORKING TIME: 30 MINUTES
TOTAL TIME: 40 MINUTES

It's the city of Buffalo—not the woolly beast of the Great Plains—that lends this dish its name. The salad was inspired by the hot-and-spicy fried chicken wings, created in upstate New York, that are known as Buffalo wings. The wings are traditionally served with celery sticks and blue-cheese dressing, and we've included both in the salad.

4 ounces semolina or Italian bread, cut into ½-inch-thick slices

2 cloves garlic, halved

1 cup reduced-sodium chicken broth, defatted

½ teaspoon dried oregano

¼ teaspoon freshly ground black pepper

¾ pound skinless, boneless chicken breasts

1¼ cups low-fat (1.5 %) buttermilk

2 tablespoons reduced-fat mayonnaise

¾ teaspoon hot pepper sauce

½ cup crumbled blue cheese (2 ounces)

3 carrots, cut into 2 x ¼-inch julienne strips

3 ribs celery, cut into 2 x ¼-inch julienne strips

4 cups mixed torn greens

1. Preheat the broiler. Broil the bread 4 inches from the heat for 2 minutes, turning once, until crisp and lightly browned. Rub the bread with the garlic, then cut the bread into ½-inch cubes.

2. Meanwhile, in a large skillet combine the broth, oregano, pepper, and 1 cup of water and bring to a boil over medium heat. Reduce to a simmer, add the chicken, cover, and cook, turning once, until the chicken is cooked through, about 10 minutes. With a slotted spoon, transfer the chicken to a plate. When cool enough to handle, shred the chicken with your fingers.

3. In a large bowl, combine the buttermilk, mayonnaise, and hot pepper sauce. Add the blue cheese, stirring to combine. Add the carrots, celery, chicken, and bread cubes, tossing to combine. Place the greens on 4 plates, top with the chicken salad, and serve warm, at room temperature, or chilled.

Helpful hints: Although blue cheese is a classic ingredient in the sauce served with Buffalo wings, you could use feta cheese instead. A combination of red and green leaf lettuces works nicely with this salad.

FAT: 9G/24%
CALORIES: 332
SATURATED FAT: 4.2G
CARBOHYDRATE: 31G
PROTEIN: 31G
CHOLESTEROL: 65MG
SODIUM: 740MG

CHICKEN TACO SALAD

SERVES: 4
WORKING TIME: 25 MINUTES
TOTAL TIME: 35 MINUTES

A fast-food taco salad may have more than 60 grams of fat! Do yourself a favor and prepare this one at home, instead.

¾ pound skinless, boneless chicken breasts
¾ teaspoon salt
¾ teaspoon ground cumin
¾ teaspoon ground coriander
¾ teaspoon dried oregano
Eight 6-inch corn tortillas
½ cup diced avocado
½ cup plain nonfat yogurt
2 tablespoons fresh lemon juice
2 tomatoes, coarsely chopped
1½ cups frozen corn kernels, thawed
6 cups shredded iceberg lettuce
2 tablespoons thinly sliced scallions

1. Preheat the broiler. Sprinkle the chicken with ¼ teaspoon each of the salt, cumin, coriander, and oregano. Broil 6 inches from the heat for 4 minutes per side, or until just cooked through. When cool enough to handle, slice the chicken crosswise into ¼-inch slices. Reduce the oven temperature to 400°. Bake the tortillas for 7 minutes, or until crisp.

2. Meanwhile, in a food processor, combine the avocado, yogurt, lemon juice, and ¼ teaspoon each of the cumin, coriander, and oregano and process until smooth. In a medium bowl, combine the tomatoes, corn, the remaining ½ teaspoon salt, and remaining ¼ teaspoon each cumin, coriander, and oregano.

3. Divide the tortillas among 4 plates. Top each tortilla with lettuce and then the tomato-corn mixture. Place the sliced chicken on top. Drizzle the avocado dressing over, sprinkle with the scallions, and serve.

Helpful hint: You can prepare the salad components up to 12 hours in advance; don't bake the tortillas or assemble the salad until just before serving.

FAT: 6G/16%
CALORIES: 338
SATURATED FAT: 1.1G
CARBOHYDRATE: 47G
PROTEIN: 28G
CHOLESTEROL: 50MG
SODIUM: 587MG

BEEF, PORK & LAMB
2

Dishes called "lo mein" traditionally consist of noodles that have been stir-fried, then combined with vegetables, meat, or seafood, and a savory sauce. Frying the noodles adds quite a bit of fat, so we've eliminated that step. In our version, pasta is tossed with juicy broiled beef strips and a sesame-peanut dressing with a delicious gingery kick.

Beef Lo Mein Salad

Serves: 4
Working time: 25 minutes
Total time: 35 minutes

8 ounces linguine or spaghetti

3-inch piece fresh ginger

3 tablespoons reduced-sodium soy sauce

2 tablespoons rice vinegar

4 teaspoons dark Oriental sesame oil

1 tablespoon honey

2 teaspoons creamy peanut butter

½ teaspoon salt

¼ teaspoon cayenne pepper

1 yellow bell pepper, cut into ¼-inch-wide strips

1 red bell pepper, cut into ¼-inch-wide strips

1 cucumber, peeled, halved lengthwise, seeded, and cut into 2 x ¼-inch strips

2 scallions, thinly sliced

¼ cup chopped fresh cilantro or parsley

10 ounces well-trimmed top round of beef

1. In a large pot of boiling water, cook the pasta until just tender. Drain well.

2. Meanwhile, preheat the broiler. Grate the ginger into a small bowl (see tip, top photo). Squeeze the ginger to extract as much ginger juice as possible (bottom photo), discarding the solids; you should have about 2 tablespoons of juice. Transfer the ginger juice to a large bowl. Whisk in the soy sauce, vinegar, sesame oil, honey, peanut butter, salt, and cayenne until smooth. Stir in the bell peppers, cucumber, scallions, and cilantro. Add the pasta, tossing well to combine.

3. Broil the beef 6 inches from the heat for about 4 minutes per side, or until medium-rare. Place the beef on a plate and let it stand for 10 minutes. Thinly slice the beef on the diagonal, reserving any juices on the plate. Transfer the beef and juices to the bowl with the pasta, tossing to combine. Serve warm, at room temperature, or chilled.

Helpful hint: If you have a cutting board with a channel or lip to collect the juices, you can transfer the beef to your cutting board, rather than a plate, to let it stand for 10 minutes before slicing.

Fat: 9g/20%
Calories: 402
Saturated Fat: 1.8g
Carbohydrate: 54g
Protein: 26g
Cholesterol: 40mg
Sodium: 783mg

To make ginger juice, grate the unpeeled fresh ginger on the fine side of a grater. Then scoop up a palm-size amount of the ginger and squeeze it—first in the palm of your hand, then between your fingers—to release the juice.

Bacon, lettuce, and tomato is such a simple, perfect combination that it's a shame to limit it to sandwiches. Our variation is a hearty potato salad with strips of lean Canadian bacon, crisp iceberg lettuce, tomato wedges, and a tangy yogurt-mayonnaise dressing. To honor its origin as a sandwich, serve the salad with white or whole-grain toast.

BACON, LETTUCE, AND TOMATO SALAD

SERVES: 4
WORKING TIME: 20 MINUTES
TOTAL TIME: 45 MINUTES

1½ pounds red potatoes or other boiling potatoes

¼ cup white wine vinegar

¼ cup reduced-sodium chicken broth, defatted

3 scallions, thinly sliced

¼ teaspoon salt

¼ teaspoon freshly ground black pepper

¾ cup plain nonfat yogurt

2 tablespoons reduced-fat mayonnaise

6 ounces Canadian bacon, cut into 2 x ¼-inch strips

2 tomatoes, cut into 8 wedges each

1 red onion, halved and thinly sliced

8 cups roughly torn iceberg lettuce

1. In a large pot of boiling water, cook the potatoes until tender, about 20 minutes. Drain well.

2. Meanwhile, in a large bowl, whisk together the vinegar, broth, scallions, salt, and pepper. When the potatoes are cool enough to handle, peel them (see tip) and cut them into ¼-inch-thick rounds. Transfer the potatoes to the bowl with the vinegar mixture, tossing well to combine. Let stand for 20 minutes.

3. Add the yogurt and mayonnaise to the potatoes and gently toss to combine. Add the Canadian bacon, tomatoes, onion, and lettuce and toss again. Divide among 4 plates and serve at room temperature or chilled.

Helpful hint: You can cook the potatoes and toss them with the vinegar mixture up to 4 hours in advance.

TIP

It's easy to peel boiled potatoes: Score the potato with a paring knife and catch a bit of the peel between the knife blade and your thumb; then just pull off the strip of peel.

FAT: 5G/15%
CALORIES: 292
SATURATED FAT: 1.3G
CARBOHYDRATE: 45G
PROTEIN: 17G
CHOLESTEROL: 22MG
SODIUM: 897MG

Italian Beef Salad

SERVES: 4
WORKING TIME: 30 MINUTES
TOTAL TIME: 30 MINUTES

With its pasta, tomatoes, green beans, and its sassy dressing—a blend of balsamic vinegar, olive oil, and fresh basil—this salad is brimming with Italian character. The broad shavings of cheese that top the salad are another authentic touch: You can cut the Parmesan shavings with a swivel-bladed vegetable peeler or a sharp paring knife.

8 ounces penne pasta

10-ounce package frozen Italian green beans, thawed

4 teaspoons olive oil

¾ pound well-trimmed sirloin, cut into 2 x ¼-inch strips

1 onion, finely chopped

3 cloves garlic, minced

1 carrot, halved lengthwise and thinly sliced

1½ pounds tomatoes, finely chopped

½ cup chopped fresh basil

2 tablespoons balsamic vinegar

½ teaspoon salt

2 ounces shaved Parmesan cheese

1. In a large pot of boiling water, cook the pasta until just tender. Add the green beans during the last 2 minutes of cooking time. Drain well.

2. Meanwhile, in a large nonstick skillet, heat the oil until hot but not smoking over medium heat. Add the beef and cook, stirring frequently, until no longer pink, about 3 minutes. With a slotted spoon, transfer the beef to a plate.

3. Add the onion and garlic to the pan and cook, stirring frequently, until the onion is tender, about 5 minutes. Add the carrot and cook, stirring frequently, until the carrot is crisp-tender, about 4 minutes. Transfer the vegetables to a large bowl and add the tomatoes, basil, vinegar, and salt.

4. Add the pasta, green beans, and beef to the bowl, tossing well to coat. Cool to room temperature, divide evenly among 4 plates, top with the Parmesan, and serve.

Helpful hint: You can make the salad up to 8 hours ahead of time; do not add the shaved Parmesan until just before serving.

FAT: 14G/24%
CALORIES: 521
SATURATED FAT: 4.9G
CARBOHYDRATE: 65G
PROTEIN: 35G
CHOLESTEROL: 63MG
SODIUM: 617MG

Spring Lamb and Asparagus Salad

SERVES: 4
WORKING TIME: 20 MINUTES
TOTAL TIME: 30 MINUTES

1¼ pounds sweet potatoes, peeled and cut into ½-inch cubes

1 pound asparagus, tough ends trimmed, cut into 2-inch lengths

¼ cup frozen apple juice concentrate

¼ cup reduced-sodium chicken broth, defatted

1 tablespoon rice vinegar

1 tablespoon Dijon mustard

2 teaspoons olive oil

½ teaspoon ground ginger

¾ teaspoon salt

1 red bell pepper, cut into 1-inch squares

1 yellow bell pepper, cut into 1-inch squares

¾ pound well-trimmed boneless lamb shoulder

4 cups arugula or watercress, tough stems removed

1. In a large pot of boiling water, cook the sweet potatoes until almost tender, about 8 minutes. Add the asparagus and cook until the asparagus are crisp-tender and the sweet potatoes are tender, about 2 minutes. Drain well.

2. Meanwhile, in a large bowl, combine the apple juice concentrate, broth, vinegar, mustard, oil, ginger, and ½ teaspoon of the salt. Add the sweet potatoes, asparagus, and bell peppers, tossing to coat.

3. Preheat the broiler. Sprinkle the lamb with the remaining ¼ teaspoon salt and broil 6 inches from the heat for about 4 minutes per side, or until medium. Place the lamb on a plate and let it stand for 10 minutes. Cut the lamb into 1 x ¼-inch strips, reserving any juices on the plate. Add the lamb and juices to the bowl along with the arugula and toss well. Divide among 4 plates and serve warm, at room temperature, or chilled.

Helpful hints: The salad may be prepared up to 1 day in advance; do not add the arugula until just before serving. Chicory or escarole, torn into bite-size pieces, may be substituted for the arugula or watercress.

FAT: 10G/27%
CALORIES: 331
SATURATED FAT: 3G
CARBOHYDRATE: 38G
PROTEIN: 22G
CHOLESTEROL: 58MG
SODIUM: 627MG

Among the tastiest signs of spring is plump asparagus. California asparagus may appear on the market as early as February, and happily for those who love this vegetable, its growing season extends well into the summer. The lush taste of lamb is a perfect match for asparagus. In this salad, sweet potatoes add substance and arugula provides a tart counterpoint to the rich flavors.

Ham and Lentil Salad

SERVES: 4
WORKING TIME: 20 MINUTES
TOTAL TIME: 50 MINUTES

L*entils are a fine foil for the smokiness of Virginia ham. The lentils and potatoes cook in the same pot, saving both time and energy.*

2 cups reduced-sodium chicken broth, defatted

4 cloves garlic, minced

1 carrot, quartered lengthwise and thinly sliced

1 cup lentils, rinsed and picked over

¾ pound red potatoes, cut into ½-inch cubes

⅓ cup fresh lemon juice

3 tablespoons cider vinegar

4 teaspoons olive oil

½ teaspoon freshly ground black pepper

¼ teaspoon salt

2 Granny Smith apples, cored and cut into ½-inch chunks

4 scallions, thinly sliced

6 cups mixed torn greens

5 ounces Virginia or Black Forest ham, in one piece, cut into 1½ x ½-inch slices

1. In a medium saucepan, bring the broth and 1 cup of water to a boil over medium heat. Add the garlic, carrot, and lentils; reduce to a simmer, cover, and cook for 10 minutes. Add the potatoes, cover, and cook until the potatoes and lentils are tender, about 20 minutes.

2. Meanwhile, in a large bowl, combine the lemon juice, vinegar, oil, pepper, and salt. Add the lentil mixture, the apples, and scallions, tossing well to combine. Cool to room temperature. Divide the greens among 4 bowls, top with the salad mixture and ham, and serve at room temperature or chilled.

Helpful hint: The dressed salad mixture can be made up to 8 hours in advance; do not add the ham or place the salad on the greens until just before serving.

FAT: 9G/19%
CALORIES: 428
SATURATED FAT: 1.8G
CARBOHYDRATE: 64G
PROTEIN: 27G
CHOLESTEROL: 21MG
SODIUM: 979MG

ZUCCHINI AND BROILED BEEF SALAD

SERVES: 4
WORKING TIME: 25 MINUTES
TOTAL TIME: 40 MINUTES

1 red bell pepper, slivered

1 zucchini, halved lengthwise and thinly sliced

¼ cup red wine or balsamic vinegar

¼ cup reduced-sodium chicken broth, defatted

2 teaspoons olive oil

¼ cup finely chopped onion

¾ teaspoon salt

¾ teaspoon dried oregano

¼ teaspoon freshly ground black pepper

¾ pound well-trimmed top round of beef

2 slices (1 ounce each) Italian bread

2 cloves garlic, peeled and halved

6 cups mixed torn greens

1. In a large vegetable steamer, steam the bell pepper and zucchini until crisp-tender, about 4 minutes. Meanwhile, in a large bowl, combine the vinegar, broth, oil, onion, ½ teaspoon of the salt, ½ teaspoon of the oregano, and the black pepper. Transfer the cooked vegetables to the bowl with the vinegar mixture, tossing to combine.

2. Meanwhile, preheat the broiler. Rub the beef with the remaining ¼ teaspoon salt and remaining ¼ teaspoon oregano. Broil the beef 6 inches from the heat for about 4 minutes per side, or until medium-rare. For the last 2 minutes of broiling, add the bread and broil for about 1 minute per side, or until lightly browned.

3. Place the beef on a plate and let it stand for 10 minutes. Thinly slice the beef on the diagonal into 1-inch pieces, reserving any juices on the plate. Transfer the beef and juices to the bowl with the vegetables, tossing to combine. Rub the garlic over the toasted bread, then cut the bread into 1-inch squares. Divide the greens evenly among 4 plates. Top with the beef mixture, place the garlic bread croutons on top, and serve warm, at room temperature, or chilled.

Helpful hint: The meat and vegetable mixture can be made up to 4 hours in advance; do not assemble the rest of the salad until just before serving.

FAT: 6G/26%
CALORIES: 210
SATURATED FAT: 1.5G
CARBOHYDRATE: 14G
PROTEIN: 24G
CHOLESTEROL: 54MG
SODIUM: 583MG

A sort of steak sandwich in a bowl, this salad brings together broiled beef, Italian bread, and vegetables.

BEEF, MUSHROOM, AND RICE SALAD

SERVES: 4
WORKING TIME: 25 MINUTES
TOTAL TIME: 35 MINUTES

A rice pilaf of sorts, redolent with the rich fragrance of fresh shiitake mushrooms, is the starting point for this meaty salad. The herbed rice is tossed with slices of broiled steak, bright bell peppers, button mushrooms, and a light vinaigrette. In the unlikely event that you end up with leftovers, enjoy them as a take-along lunch the next day.

1½ cups reduced-sodium chicken broth, defatted

1 cup long-grain rice

4 ounces shiitake or button mushrooms, trimmed and thinly sliced

4 scallions, thinly sliced

1 teaspoon salt

¼ teaspoon dried thyme

½ teaspoon dried rosemary, crumbled

¾ pound well-trimmed sirloin

¼ cup red wine vinegar

1 tablespoon olive oil

1 green bell pepper, cut into ¼-inch squares

1 red bell pepper, cut into ¼-inch squares

6 ounces button mushrooms, thinly sliced

4 cups mesclun or mixed torn greens

1. In a medium saucepan, bring 1 cup of the broth and 1¼ cups of water to a boil. Stir in the rice, shiitake mushrooms, scallions, ¼ teaspoon of the salt, the thyme, and rosemary. Reduce to a simmer, cover, and cook until the rice is tender, about 17 minutes.

2. Meanwhile, preheat the broiler. Sprinkle the beef with ¼ teaspoon of the salt and broil 6 inches from the heat for about 4 minutes per side, or until medium-rare. Place the beef on a plate and let it stand for 10 minutes. Thinly slice the beef on the diagonal into 1-inch pieces, reserving any juices on the plate.

3. In a large bowl, combine the beef juices, vinegar, oil, the remaining ½ cup broth, and remaining ½ teaspoon salt. Add the rice mixture to the dressing along with the bell peppers and fluff with a fork to combine. Cool to room temperature, then stir in the beef and button mushrooms. Place the greens in a bowl or on a platter, top with the rice mixture, and serve at room temperature or chilled.

Helpful hint: The rice salad may be prepared up to 8 hours in advance; do not place the salad on the greens until just before serving.

FAT: 9G/22%
CALORIES: 372
SATURATED FAT: 2.4G
CARBOHYDRATE: 46G
PROTEIN: 27G
CHOLESTEROL: 57MG
SODIUM: 819MG

Melon
and tomato bring
lively flavor and eye-
catching color to this
appealing main dish.
Cool cucumber (a close
relative of melon) and
crisp water chestnuts
add textural interest.
The lean tenderloin
of pork is rubbed with
a chili-ginger spice
blend before roasting;
the dressing includes
more of the same
spices, plus the pork's
well-seasoned juices.

SUMMER PORK SALAD WITH MELON

SERVES: 4
WORKING TIME: 15 MINUTES
TOTAL TIME: 50 MINUTES

1½ teaspoons chili powder

¾ teaspoon ground ginger

¾ teaspoon salt

¾ teaspoon sugar

¾ pound well-trimmed pork tenderloin

¼ cup fresh lime juice

1 tablespoon olive oil

Half a cantaloupe, seeded, peeled, and cut into ½-inch chunks (see tip)

1 tomato, cut into 8 wedges

1 cucumber, peeled, halved lengthwise, seeded, and thinly sliced

1 cup frozen corn kernels, thawed

½ cup canned sliced water chestnuts

4 cups mixed torn greens

1. Preheat the oven to 425°. In a small bowl, combine the chili powder, ginger, ¼ teaspoon of the salt, and the sugar. Place the pork on a rack in a roasting pan and rub 1 teaspoon of the spice mixture into it. Roast the pork for about 25 minutes, or until cooked through but still juicy. Place the pork on a plate and let it stand for 10 minutes. Cut the pork crosswise into ¼-inch-thick slices, reserving any juices on the plate.

2. In a large bowl, combine the pork juices, lime juice, oil, the remaining 2¼ teaspoons spice mixture, remaining ½ teaspoon salt, and 2 tablespoons of water. Add the pork, cantaloupe, tomato, cucumber, corn, water chestnuts, and greens, tossing well to combine. Divide among 4 plates and serve warm, at room temperature, or chilled.

Helpful hints: This salad is best served soon after it's made; the liquid from the cucumber and tomatoes may thin the dressing if it stands too long. If you have a cutting board with a channel or lip to collect the meat juices, you can transfer the pork to your cutting board, rather than a plate, to let it stand for 10 minutes before slicing.

Here's an easy way to cut up a cantaloupe: Halve and seed the melon, then cut it into slender wedges. To peel the melon wedges, run a knife between the flesh and rind; then cut crosswise into chunks.

FAT: 7G/26%
CALORIES: 241
SATURATED FAT: 1.6G
CARBOHYDRATE: 25G
PROTEIN: 22G
CHOLESTEROL: 50MG
SODIUM: 491MG

BEEF AND BROCCOLI WITH MUSTARD VINAIGRETTE

SERVES: 4
WORKING TIME: 20 MINUTES
TOTAL TIME: 30 MINUTES

Although the resemblance is not immediately apparent, broccoli and mustard come from the same plant family. Perhaps that's why broccoli is so tasty with a mustard vinaigrette. Even with no botanical kinship, however, the salad's other ingredients—potatoes, carrots, bell pepper, and juicy squares of sirloin steak—take equally well to the Dijon dressing.

⅓ cup red wine vinegar

⅓ cup reduced-sodium chicken broth, defatted

2 tablespoons Dijon mustard

1 tablespoon plus 2 teaspoons olive oil

½ teaspoon dried tarragon

¼ teaspoon salt

4 teaspoons capers, rinsed and drained

3 cups broccoli florets

1½ pounds all-purpose potatoes, peeled and cut into ½-inch cubes

1 cup peeled baby carrots

1 red bell pepper, cut into ½-inch squares

¾ pound well-trimmed sirloin

1. In a large bowl, combine the vinegar, broth, 1 tablespoon of the mustard, the oil, tarragon, and salt. Add the capers, stirring to combine.

2. In a large pot of boiling water, cook the broccoli for 1 minute to blanch. With a slotted spoon, remove the broccoli and set aside. Add the potatoes and carrots to the water, return to a boil, and cook until the potatoes are tender, about 7 minutes. Drain well. Add the potatoes, carrots, and bell pepper to the bowl with the vinegar mixture, tossing to combine.

3. Meanwhile, preheat the broiler. Brush the beef with the remaining 1 tablespoon mustard and broil 6 inches from the heat for about 4 minutes per side, or until medium-rare. Place the beef on a plate and let it stand for 10 minutes. Thinly slice the beef on the diagonal, then cut it into 1-inch squares, reserving any juices on the plate. Add the beef, beef juices, and broccoli to the bowl with the vegetables. Serve warm, at room temperature, or chilled.

Helpful hint: The salad can be made up to 8 hours in advance; don't add the blanched broccoli until just before serving.

FAT: 11G/29%
CALORIES: 342
SATURATED FAT: 2.7G
CARBOHYDRATE: 34G
PROTEIN: 26G
CHOLESTEROL: 57MG
SODIUM: 548MG

Ham and Sweet Potato Salad

SERVES: 4
WORKING TIME: 15 MINUTES
TOTAL TIME: 40 MINUTES

1½ pounds sweet potatoes, peeled, halved lengthwise, and cut crosswise into ½-inch-thick half-rounds

½ cup reduced-sodium chicken broth, defatted

¼ cup white wine vinegar

1 tablespoon Dijon mustard

1 tablespoon capers, rinsed and drained

½ teaspoon salt

2 tablespoons reduced-fat mayonnaise

6 ounces sliced reduced-sodium smoked ham, cut into thin strips

2 yellow or red bell peppers, cut into thin strips

1 cucumber, peeled, halved lengthwise, seeded, and thinly sliced

1 bunch of watercress, tough stems removed

1. In a large pot of boiling water, cook the sweet potatoes until tender, about 10 minutes. Drain well.

2. Meanwhile, in a large bowl, combine the broth, vinegar, mustard, capers, and salt. Add the sweet potatoes, tossing to coat. Let stand for 20 minutes.

3. Add the mayonnaise, ham, bell peppers, cucumber, and watercress, tossing well to combine. Divide among 4 plates and serve at room temperature or chilled.

Helpful hint: You can make the salad up to 8 hours in advance; do not add the watercress until just before serving.

FAT: 3G/12%
CALORIES: 225
SATURATED FAT: 0.8G
CARBOHYDRATE: 38G
PROTEIN: 11G
CHOLESTEROL: 20MG
SODIUM: 938MG

We've taken the time-honored Southern meal of ham, sweet potatoes, and greens and transformed it into a salad with rich, distinct flavors. We replaced the traditional slow-simmered collards or mustard greens with tart fresh watercress, and added a piquant dressing. Corn bread is the perfect partner for this salad; or try corn sticks made with Cheddar and chives.

Rice Salad with Lamb and Apples

Serves: 4
Working time: 30 minutes
Total time: 1 hour

This Indian-inspired salad, with its curry-rubbed lamb and yogurt-chutney dressing, is an especially good make-ahead choice.

1 cup long-grain rice

3 cloves garlic, minced

½ teaspoon salt

1½ cups frozen peas

2 teaspoons curry powder

½ teaspoon ground ginger

½ teaspoon sugar

¾ pound well-trimmed boneless lamb shoulder chops

1 cup plain nonfat yogurt

¼ cup mango chutney, chopped if chunky

1 red apple, cored and cut into ½-inch chunks

1 green apple, cored and cut into ½-inch chunks

1 yellow summer squash, quartered lengthwise and cut into ½-inch slices

1. In a medium saucepan, bring 2¼ cups of water to a boil. Add the rice, garlic, and ¼ teaspoon of the salt, reduce to a simmer, cover, and cook until the rice is tender, about 17 minutes. Add the peas, transfer to a large bowl, fluff with a fork, and set aside to cool to room temperature.

2. Meanwhile, preheat the broiler. In a small bowl, combine the curry powder, ginger, and sugar. Rub 1½ teaspoons of the spice mixture into the lamb. Broil the lamb 6 inches from the heat for about 4 minutes per side, or until medium. Place the lamb on a plate and let it stand for 10 minutes. Cut the lamb into 1 x ¼-inch-thick strips, reserving any juices on the plate.

3. In a small bowl, combine the lamb juices, yogurt, chutney, the remaining 1½ teaspoons spice mixture, and the remaining ¼ teaspoon salt. Add to the bowl with the rice along with the lamb, apples, and squash. Toss to combine and let stand at room temperature for 30 minutes before dividing among 4 bowls and serving.

Helpful hint: The salad can be made up to 8 hours in advance. Bring to room temperature before serving.

Fat: 7g/13%
Calories: 483
Saturated Fat: 2.3g
Carbohydrate: 77g
Protein: 27g
Cholesterol: 57mg
Sodium: 611mg

Salmagundi Salad

Serves: 4
Working time: 25 minutes
Total time: 35 minutes

1½ pounds small red potatoes, quartered

1½ cups low-fat (1.5%) buttermilk

3 tablespoons reduced-fat mayonnaise

3 tablespoons fresh lemon juice

1 teaspoon paprika

½ teaspoon salt

½ teaspoon sugar

¾ pound well-trimmed top round of beef, 1½ inches thick

½ teaspoon dried thyme

¼ teaspoon freshly ground black pepper

4 cups finely shredded red cabbage

4 scallions, thinly sliced

2 ribs celery, thinly sliced

1. In a large pot of boiling water, cook the potatoes until tender, about 15 minutes. Drain well.

2. Meanwhile, in a large bowl, combine the buttermilk, mayonnaise, lemon juice, paprika, salt, and sugar. Add the potatoes and toss to coat.

3. Preheat the broiler. Sprinkle the beef with the thyme and pepper and broil 6 inches from the heat for about 4 minutes per side, or until medium-rare. Transfer the beef to a plate and let stand for 10 minutes. Cut the beef into 1 x ¼-inch-thick strips, reserving any juices on the plate.

4. Add the cabbage, scallions, and celery to the bowl with the potatoes, tossing to combine. Add the beef and beef juices and toss again. Divide among 4 plates and serve warm, at room temperature, or chilled.

Helpful hint: If the potatoes are very small, you can halve them; if you can only get large potatoes, cut them into 6 or 8 wedges each.

Fat: 8G/20%
Calories: 362
Saturated Fat: 2.4G
Carbohydrate: 45G
Protein: 28G
Cholesterol: 59MG
Sodium: 490MG

All *sorts of chopped or diced foods can go into a salmagundi. We've used beef, potatoes, and vegetables.*

SPICED BEEF WITH CREAMY MANGO DRESSING

SERVES: 4
WORKING TIME: 20 MINUTES
TOTAL TIME: 30 MINUTES

The sweet-and-spicy seasonings that flavor the steak here are a Caribbean inspiration —a simplified version of the spice mixture rubbed on Jamaican jerk chicken. The spiced beef is just one attraction in this salad made with sweet sugar snap peas, cherry tomatoes, and crunchy water chestnuts. Mixed torn greens and warm pita wedges round out the dish.

¾ pound well-trimmed sirloin
½ teaspoon salt
¼ teaspoon sugar
¼ teaspoon freshly ground black pepper
⅛ teaspoon ground allspice
3 tablespoons fresh lime juice
Two 8-inch pita breads, cut into 6 wedges each
½ pound sugar snap peas or snow peas, strings removed
⅓ cup mango chutney, chopped if chunky
¼ cup reduced-fat sour cream
2 cups cherry tomatoes, halved
½ cup canned sliced water chestnuts, or ½ cup diced celery
3 scallions, thinly sliced
4 cups mixed torn greens

1. Preheat the broiler. Sprinkle the beef with ¼ teaspoon of the salt, the sugar, pepper, and allspice. Sprinkle 1 tablespoon of the lime juice over and broil 6 inches from the heat for about 4 minutes per side, or until medium-rare. Leave the broiler on. Place the beef on a plate and let it stand for 10 minutes. Thinly slice the beef on the diagonal, reserving any juices on the plate.

2. Meanwhile, broil the pitas wedges for about 1 minute per side, or until lightly crisped. In a medium saucepan of boiling water, cook the sugar snap peas for 1 minute to blanch. Drain well.

3. In a large bowl, combine the chutney, sour cream, the remaining 2 tablespoons lime juice, the beef juices, and 2 tablespoons of water. Add the beef, the sugar snap peas, tomatoes, water chestnuts, scallions, and the remaining ¼ teaspoon salt, tossing to combine. Divide the greens evenly among 4 plates. Top with the meat mixture, place the pita wedges alongside, and serve warm, at room temperature, or chilled.

Helpful hint: The beef-and-vegetable mixture can be made up to 8 hours in advance; do not warm the pita wedges or place the salad on the greens until just before serving.

FAT: 8G/17%
CALORIES: 432
SATURATED FAT: 2.9G
CARBOHYDRATE: 62G
PROTEIN: 29G
CHOLESTEROL: 62MG
SODIUM: 890MG

*T*he standard spinach salad, with its mushrooms, bacon, and hard-cooked eggs, seems old-fashioned when compared with this vibrant blend of vegetables, beef, and citrus. Warm potatoes bathed in a mustard vinaigrette are tossed with herbed steak, spinach, oranges, bell pepper, and olives. Serve the salad with bread so you don't miss a drop of the dressing.

Beef, Spinach, and Orange Salad

Serves: 4
Working time: 25 minutes
Total time: 50 minutes

1½ pounds all-purpose potatoes

¼ cup red wine vinegar

4 teaspoons Dijon mustard

1 tablespoon olive oil

¾ teaspoon salt

⅛ teaspoon cayenne pepper

¾ pound well-trimmed top round of beef or beef sirloin, 1½ inches thick

½ teaspoon dried oregano

¼ teaspoon freshly ground black pepper

2 scallions, very thinly sliced

¼ cup brine- or oil-cured black olives, pitted and slivered

2 navel oranges, peeled and sectioned (see tip)

1 red bell pepper, cut into thin slices

6 cups packed fresh spinach leaves (about 9 ounces), torn

1. In a large pot of boiling water, cook the potatoes until tender, about 20 minutes. Drain well.

2. Meanwhile, in a large bowl, whisk together the vinegar, mustard, oil, ½ teaspoon of the salt, and the cayenne. When the potatoes are cool enough to handle, peel them and cut them into 1-inch chunks. Transfer the potatoes to the bowl with the vinegar mixture, tossing well to combine.

3. Preheat the broiler. Rub the beef with the remaining ¼ teaspoon salt, the oregano, and black pepper. Broil 6 inches from the heat for about 4 minutes per side, or until medium-rare. Place the beef on a plate and let it stand for 10 minutes. Cut the beef into 1 x ¼-inch-thick strips, reserving any juices on the plate.

4. Add the beef, beef juices, scallions, olives, orange sections, bell pepper, and spinach to the bowl with the potatoes. Toss well, divide among 4 plates, and serve at room temperature.

Helpful hint: If you have a cutting board with a channel or lip to collect the juices, you can transfer the beef to your cutting board, rather than a plate, to let it stand for 10 minutes before slicing.

TIP

To prepare the oranges, remove the peels and, using a small knife, trim away all the bitter white pith. Working over a sieve set over a bowl to catch the juices, cut between the membranes to release the orange sections. Save the juices for another use.

Fat: 8g/21%
Calories: 350
Saturated Fat: 1.7g
Carbohydrate: 44g
Protein: 26g
Cholesterol: 54mg
Sodium: 704mg

ROAST PORK AND SWEET POTATO SALAD

SERVES: 4
WORKING TIME: 20 MINUTES
TOTAL TIME: 45 MINUTES

If you were to buy roast pork at a Chinatown market, you'd get a thick slab of meat heavily glazed with honey, ginger, soy sauce, and spices. The succulent slices of pork tenderloin in this salad have a similar flavor, but the meat is brushed with a light orange-soy mixture before roasting. Mellow sweet potatoes and sweet sugar snap peas are good companions for the pork.

3 tablespoons reduced-sodium soy sauce
3 tablespoons frozen orange juice concentrate
4 teaspoons firmly packed dark brown sugar
¼ teaspoon ground ginger
⅛ teaspoon ground allspice
¾ pound well-trimmed pork tenderloin
1 pound sweet potatoes, peeled and cut lengthwise into 8 wedges each
6 ounces sugar snap peas or snow peas, strings removed
¼ cup balsamic vinegar
2 teaspoons olive oil
1 red onion, finely chopped
6 cups mixed torn greens

1. Preheat the oven to 425°. In a large bowl, combine the soy sauce, orange juice concentrate, brown sugar, ginger, and allspice. Measure out 1 tablespoon of the soy mixture to use as a baste.

2. Place the pork on a rack in a roasting pan and brush the pork with the reserved 1 tablespoon soy mixture. Roast for about 25 minutes, or until the pork is cooked through but still juicy. Place the pork on a plate and let it stand for 10 minutes. Slice the pork into ¼-inch-thick slices, reserving any juices on the plate.

3. Meanwhile, in a medium pot of boiling water, cook the sweet potatoes until tender, about 8 minutes. Add the sugar snap peas for the last 1 minute of cooking time. Drain well.

4. Whisk the pork juices, vinegar, and oil into the soy mixture in the bowl. Add the pork, sweet potatoes, sugar snaps, and onion, tossing well to combine. Divide the greens among 4 plates, top with the salad mixture, and serve warm, at room temperature, or chilled.

Helpful hints: The salad can be made up to 8 hours in a advance; do not place it over the greens until just before serving.

FAT: 7G/19%
CALORIES: 326
SATURATED FAT: 1.8G
CARBOHYDRATE: 42G
PROTEIN: 25G
CHOLESTEROL: 60MG
SODIUM: 564MG

FLORENTINE BEEF SALAD

SERVES: 4
WORKING TIME: 20 MINUTES
TOTAL TIME: 50 MINUTES

They say that the best steaks in Italy are served in Florence. The term "Florentine" is also applied to dishes made with spinach.

½ cup sun-dried (not oil-packed) tomatoes

4 cloves garlic, peeled

1 pound fresh tomatoes, quartered, or 2 cups no-salt-added canned tomatoes, drained

½ cup reduced-sodium chicken broth, defatted

2 tablespoons balsamic or red wine vinegar

1 tablespoon olive oil

½ teaspoon salt

1½ pounds all-purpose potatoes, quartered

¾ pound well-trimmed top round of beef

½ pound mushrooms, thinly sliced

4 scallions, thinly sliced

6 cups packed fresh spinach leaves (about 9 ounces), torn into bite-size pieces

1. In a small saucepan of boiling water, cook the sun-dried tomatoes for 5 minutes to soften, adding the garlic during the last 2 minutes of cooking time. Drain, transfer to a food processor along with the fresh tomatoes, broth, vinegar, oil, and ¼ teaspoon of the salt and process to a smooth purée. Transfer the dressing to a large bowl.

2. In a large pot of boiling water, cook the potatoes until tender, about 20 minutes. Drain well. When cool enough to handle, peel the potatoes, cut them into thin slices, and transfer them to the bowl with the dressing.

3. Meanwhile, preheat the broiler. Sprinkle the beef with the remaining ¼ teaspoon salt and broil 6 inches from the heat for about 4 minutes per side, or until medium-rare. Place the beef on a plate and let it stand for 10 minutes. Slice the meat on the diagonal into 1-inch-wide squares, reserving any juices on the plate.

4. Add the beef, beef juices, mushrooms, and scallions to the potatoes, tossing to coat. Add the spinach and toss again. Divide among 4 plates and serve warm, at room temperature, or chilled.

Helpful hint: The salad may be prepared up to 8 hours ahead of time; do not add the greens until just before serving.

FAT: 8G/19%
CALORIES: 373
SATURATED FAT: 1.7G
CARBOHYDRATE: 50G
PROTEIN: 30G
CHOLESTEROL: 54MG
SODIUM: 465MG

VEGETABLES

3

THREE-BEAN SALAD WITH WALNUTS

SERVES: 4
WORKING TIME: 15 MINUTES
TOTAL TIME: 20 MINUTES

2 cloves garlic, peeled

¾ pound green beans, cut into 2-inch pieces

¾ pound yellow wax beans, cut into 2-inch pieces

¾ cup plain nonfat yogurt

⅓ cup chopped fresh mint

2 tablespoons reduced-fat mayonnaise

¾ teaspoon salt

Two 16-ounce cans red kidney beans, rinsed and drained

1 cucumber, peeled, halved lengthwise, seeded, and cut into ¼-inch dice

¼ cup chopped walnuts

16 leaves Boston, Bibb, or iceberg lettuce

1. In a large pot of boiling water, cook the garlic for 2 minutes to blanch. With a slotted spoon, remove the garlic and when cool enough to handle, finely chop.

2. Add the green beans and wax beans to the boiling water and cook until crisp-tender, about 5 minutes. Drain, rinse under cold water, and drain again.

3. In a large bowl, combine the chopped garlic, yogurt, mint, mayonnaise, and salt. Fold in the green beans, wax beans, kidney beans, cucumber, and walnuts. Divide the lettuce among 4 plates, top with the bean mixture, and serve at room temperature or chilled.

Helpful hints: The salad can be made up to 8 hours in advance; don't spoon it over the lettuce or add the walnuts until just before serving. If yellow wax beans are not available, you can substitute additional fresh green beans or frozen Italian green beans, if you like.

FAT: 8G/22%
CALORIES: 321
SATURATED FAT: 0.8G
CARBOHYDRATE: 47G
PROTEIN: 19G
CHOLESTEROL: 1MG
SODIUM: 803MG

This salad is usually served as a side dish, but since its main component is kidney beans (which are high in protein), it can make a substantial main dish, too. For variety's sake, you can mix and match the canned beans you use: One can of kidney beans and one of chick-peas, for instance, would work well also. Accompany the salad with crusty rolls for a satisfying meal.

Corn on the cob has an ineffable sweetness that is hard to duplicate. Here we slice raw kernels off the cob and toss them with colorful vegetables, cubes of jack cheese, and a tangy-sweet dressing fired up with jalapeño pepper. If you haven't discovered it already, you'll find the crunchy sweetness of raw corn to be one of the delicious pleasures of summertime.

Fresh Corn Confetti Salad with Jack Cheese

Serves: 4
Working time: 20 minutes
Total time: 20 minutes

⅓ cup balsamic vinegar

2 tablespoons honey

½ teaspoon salt

1 pickled jalapeño pepper, finely chopped

4 cups fresh corn kernels (see tip), or 4 cups no-salt-added canned corn kernels, drained

2 cups cherry tomatoes, halved

2 ribs celery, thinly sliced

1 red bell pepper, cut into ½-inch squares

1 green bell pepper, cut into ½-inch squares

1 red onion, finely chopped

¼ cup chopped fresh parsley

3 ounces Monterey jack cheese, cut into ¼-inch dice

1. In a large bowl, combine the vinegar, honey, salt, and jalapeño pepper.

2. Add the corn, tomatoes, celery, bell peppers, onion, parsley, and cheese. Toss to combine and serve at room temperature or chilled.

Helpful hints: Choose fresh ears of corn with moist green stalks and plump kernels. Refrigerate the corn as soon as you get it home: Warmth hastens the conversion of its natural sugars to starch. Time also robs fresh corn of its sweetness, so use corn within a day or two of purchase. If you use canned corn, be sure to get no-salt-added, which has a fresher taste and crunchier texture than regular canned corn.

With a long, sharp knife, slice the corn kernels from the cob in strips. Then, with your fingers, break up the strips into individual kernels. You'll need about 4 medium ears of fresh corn to yield 4 cups of kernels.

Fat: 9g/28%
Calories: 290
Saturated Fat: 4g
Carbohydrate: 49g
Protein: 12g
Cholesterol: 23mg
Sodium: 496mg

Vegetable Antipasto Salad

SERVES: 4
WORKING TIME: 20 MINUTES
TOTAL TIME: 40 MINUTES PLUS CHILLING TIME

A selection of tasty tidbits enjoyed before the start of an Italian meal is called an antipasto. Vegetables—marinated, roasted, grilled, or stuffed—play a major role. For our main-course antipasto salad, we've taken potatoes, artichokes, beans, celery, and bell peppers, dressed them with an herbed balsamic vinaigrette, and tossed them with cubes of provolone.

½ cup reduced-sodium chicken broth, defatted

⅓ cup balsamic vinegar

1 tablespoon olive oil

1 teaspoon firmly packed light brown sugar

¾ teaspoon dried oregano

½ teaspoon freshly ground black pepper

¼ teaspoon salt

1 pound all-purpose potatoes

Two 9-ounce packages frozen artichoke hearts

One 19-ounce can red kidney beans, rinsed and drained

2 ribs celery, thinly sliced

1 red bell pepper, cut into ½-inch squares

1 yellow bell pepper, cut into ½-inch squares

4 ounces provolone cheese, in one piece, cut into ¼-inch dice

1. In a large bowl, combine the broth, vinegar, oil, brown sugar, oregano, black pepper, and salt.

2. In a large pot of boiling water, cook the potatoes until tender, about 25 minutes. When cool enough to handle, but still warm, peel and cut into ½-inch cubes. Add the potatoes to the broth mixture.

3. Meanwhile, in a medium saucepan of boiling water, cook the artichokes until tender, about 5 minutes. Drain well and add to the potatoes along with the beans, celery, and bell peppers, tossing to combine. Cover and refrigerate for at least 1 hour or up to 8 hours. Toss with the provolone, spoon onto 4 plates, and serve at room temperature or chilled.

Helpful hint: You can use 2 red or yellow bell peppers instead of 1 of each, if you like.

FAT: 12G/28%
CALORIES: 386
SATURATED FAT: 5.5G
CARBOHYDRATE: 52G
PROTEIN: 20G
CHOLESTEROL: 20MG
SODIUM: 705MG

Shades of green that speak of spring make this salad especially appealing. Tender lettuce, thinly sliced cucumbers, tiny peas, and snippets of scallion and dill form a refreshing backdrop for savory slivers of smoked salmon; sliced potatoes lend substance to the salad. A fitting accompaniment would be thin-sliced dark pumpernickel or rye bread.

SCANDINAVIAN SALAD

SERVES: 4
WORKING TIME: 15 MINUTES
TOTAL TIME: 40 MINUTES

1½ pounds all-purpose potatoes

3 tablespoons rice vinegar

1 cup plain nonfat yogurt

2 tablespoons reduced-fat sour cream

¾ teaspoon salt

¼ teaspoon freshly ground black pepper

1 European cucumber (see tip), unpeeled and thinly sliced

1¼ cups frozen peas, thawed

4 scallions, thinly sliced

½ cup snipped fresh dill

4 ounces thinly sliced smoked salmon, slivered

6 cups mixed greens

1. In a large pot of boiling water, cook the potatoes until tender, about 25 minutes. When cool enough to handle, but still warm, peel and cut the potatoes into ½-inch-thick rounds. Transfer to a large bowl, sprinkle the vinegar over, and gently toss to coat.

2. In a separate bowl, combine the yogurt, sour cream, salt, and pepper. Fold in the cucumber, peas, scallions, and dill. Add the potatoes, tossing to coat. Fold in the salmon.

3. Divide the greens among 4 plates, top with the potato mixture, and serve warm, at room temperature, or chilled.

Helpful hint: The salad can be made up to 8 hours in advance; don't arrange the salad over the greens until just before serving.

FAT: 3G/9%
CALORIES: 310
SATURATED FAT: 1G
CARBOHYDRATE: 56G
PROTEIN: 18G
CHOLESTEROL: 10MG
SODIUM: 810MG

TIP

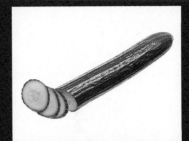

European cucumbers, also known as English, hothouse, or greenhouse cucumbers, are long (up to 2 feet), slender, and usually sold unwaxed so they don't need to be peeled. They are firm and virtually seedless, with a mild flavor. Kirby cucumbers—small "pickling" cukes—are a good substitute for European cucumbers; they're firm and crunchy with smaller seeds than regular cucumbers. Use 2 to 3 Kirbys for 1 European cucumber.

MUSHROOM BARLEY SALAD

SERVES: 4
WORKING TIME: 20 MINUTES
TOTAL TIME: 25 MINUTES

One of the lesser-used grains, barley has a rich, nutlike flavor and, like all grains, it absorbs sauces and dressings beautifully. We've combined quick-cooking barley (just as nutritious as pearl barley, but ready in about one-quarter the time) with two kinds of mushrooms, corn, and bell peppers. The garlicky mushrooms are nicely balanced by the fresh flavors of lemon and mint.

1¼ cups reduced-sodium chicken broth, defatted
1 cup quick-cooking barley
½ teaspoon salt
½ teaspoon dried thyme
3 cloves garlic, minced
¼ cup fresh lemon juice
½ pound fresh shiitake mushrooms, trimmed and thinly sliced
½ pound button mushrooms, thinly sliced
1 tablespoon olive oil
½ teaspoon freshly ground black pepper
6 scallions, thinly sliced
2 red bell peppers, cut into ½-inch squares
2 cups thawed frozen or no-salt-added canned corn kernels
½ cup chopped fresh mint or basil
1¼ cups crumbled feta cheese (5 ounces)

1. In a medium saucepan, bring 1 cup of the broth and 1 cup of water to a boil over medium heat. Add the barley, ¼ teaspoon of the salt, and the thyme. Reduce to a simmer, cover, and cook until the barley is tender, about 12 minutes.

2. Meanwhile, in a large skillet, bring the remaining ¼ cup broth, the garlic, and 1 tablespoon of the lemon juice to a boil over medium heat. Add the shiitake and button mushrooms, cover, and cook until just tender, about 5 minutes.

3. In a large bowl, combine the oil, black pepper, the remaining 3 tablespoons lemon juice, and remaining ¼ teaspoon salt. Add the barley (and its cooking liquid, if any), the mushrooms (and their cooking liquid, if any), the scallions, bell peppers, corn, and mint. Fold to combine. Divide among 4 plates, sprinkle the feta over, and serve warm, at room temperature, or chilled.

Helpful hints: The salad can be made up to 8 hours in advance; don't add the feta until just before serving. If shiitake mushrooms are not available, you can use all button mushrooms.

FAT: 13G/29%
CALORIES: 384
SATURATED FAT: 5.9G
CARBOHYDRATE: 58G
PROTEIN: 16G
CHOLESTEROL: 32MG
SODIUM: 856MG

Egg Salad with Roasted Pepper Dressing

SERVES: 4
WORKING TIME: 20 MINUTES
TOTAL TIME: 45 MINUTES

*S*ome of the egg yolks are discarded to reduce fat in this salad, but you won't miss them: We've replaced them with potatoes.

2 yellow or red bell peppers, halved lengthwise and seeded

¼ cup plain nonfat yogurt

3 tablespoons reduced-fat mayonnaise

1 teaspoon salt

½ teaspoon turmeric

3 scallions, thinly sliced

1 red bell pepper, cut into ¼-inch dice

1 pound all-purpose potatoes

5 hard-cooked eggs

6 cups mixed greens

1. Preheat the broiler. Place the yellow bell peppers, cut-sides down, on the broiler rack. Broil the peppers 4 inches from the heat for 12 minutes, or until the skins are blackened. When the peppers are cool enough to handle, remove the skins, transfer to a food processor, and process to a smooth purée. Transfer the purée to a large bowl and whisk in the yogurt, mayonnaise, salt, turmeric, scallions, and red bell pepper.

2. Meanwhile, in a large pot of boiling water, cook the potatoes until tender, about 25 minutes. When cool enough to handle, but still warm, peel and cut the potatoes into ½-inch cubes. Transfer to the bowl with the dressing.

3. Separate the hard-cooked egg whites and yolks and discard 3 of the yolks. Coarsely chop the remaining eggs and add to the bowl with the potatoes and dressing. Cover and refrigerate for at least 1 hour or as long as overnight. Divide the greens among 4 plates, spoon the egg salad over, and serve at room temperature or chilled.

Helpful hint: For perfect hard-cooked eggs, place the eggs in a saucepan, add cold water to cover by 1 inch, and bring to a boil over medium-high heat. As soon as the water comes to a boil, cover the pan, remove from the heat, and let stand for exactly 17 minutes. Peel the eggs under cold running water.

FAT: 5G/21%
CALORIES: 212
SATURATED FAT: 1.3G
CARBOHYDRATE: 31G
PROTEIN: 11G
CHOLESTEROL: 107MG
SODIUM: 737MG

APPLE-CARROT SALAD WITH YOGURT DRESSING

SERVES: 4
WORKING TIME: 20 MINUTES
TOTAL TIME: 40 MINUTES

4 cups boiling water

1 cup bulghur (cracked wheat)

1 pound carrots, thinly sliced on the diagonal

1 cup plain nonfat yogurt

½ teaspoon grated lemon zest

3 tablespoons fresh lemon juice

1 tablespoon reduced-fat mayonnaise

1 teaspoon paprika

¾ teaspoon salt

2 Granny Smith apples, cored and cut into ½-inch chunks

2 ribs celery, halved lengthwise and thinly sliced

6 cups shredded green cabbage

2 hard-cooked eggs

¼ cup coarsely chopped pecans

1. In a medium bowl, combine the boiling water and bulghur. Let stand until the bulghur has softened, about 30 minutes. Drain and squeeze dry.

2. Meanwhile, in a large pot of boiling water, cook the carrots until crisp-tender, about 7 minutes. Drain well.

3. In a large bowl, combine the yogurt, lemon zest, lemon juice, mayonnaise, paprika, and salt. Fold in the bulghur, carrots, apples, and celery.

4. Divide the cabbage evenly among 4 plates and top with the carrot mixture. Coarsely chop the eggs and sprinkle over the carrot mixture. Sprinkle the pecans over and serve warm, at room temperature, or chilled.

Helpful hint: The carrot mixture and the hard-cooked eggs can be prepared up to 1 day in advance. (Peel the eggs as soon as they're done and store them, covered, in a small bowl in the refrigerator.) Do not chop the eggs or assemble the salad until just before serving.

FAT: 9G/22%
CALORIES: 368
SATURATED FAT: 1.6G
CARBOHYDRATE: 63G
PROTEIN: 14G
CHOLESTEROL: 107MG
SODIUM: 598MG

Here's a change from the familiar carrot-raisin combination. Bulghur gives the salad body; apples add crunch.

WILTED SPINACH SALAD

SERVES: 4
WORKING TIME: 35 MINUTES
TOTAL TIME: 35 MINUTES

It's the hot vinaigrette made with bacon drippings that traditionally serves to wilt a spinach salad— making it a high-fat dish. We've saved the flavor but cut the fat (especially the saturated fat) by substituting lean Canadian bacon cooked in a little olive oil. And we've included potatoes, chick-peas, and croutons to make the salad more filling.

1½ pounds all-purpose potatoes, peeled, halved lengthwise, and cut crosswise into ¼-inch-thick half-rounds

3 ounces French bread, halved horizontally

1 red onion

2 teaspoons olive oil

½ cup diced Canadian bacon (3 ounces)

2 tablespoons flour

½ cup distilled white vinegar

2 tablespoons sugar

½ teaspoon salt

¼ teaspoon freshly ground black pepper

10 cups packed torn spinach (about 1 pound)

1 cup canned chick-peas, rinsed and drained

1. In a large pot of boiling water, cook the potatoes until tender, about 10 minutes. Drain well.

2. Meanwhile, preheat the broiler. Broil the bread 6 inches from the heat for about 1 minute per side, or until crisp and brown. When cool enough to handle, cut the bread into ½-inch chunks and place in a large bowl.

3. Halve the onion. Cut one of the halves into thin slivers and set aside. Finely chop the remaining onion half. In a medium nonstick skillet, heat the oil until hot but not smoking over medium heat. Add the Canadian bacon and cook until lightly crisped, about minutes. Add the finely chopped onion and cook, stirring frequently, until tender, about 5 minutes. Add the flour and cook, stirring, for 1 minute to coat the onions. Whisk in the vinegar, sugar, salt, and pepper and cook, stirring occasionally, until slightly thickened, about 4 minutes.

4. Add the spinach, chick-peas, slivered onion, and potatoes to the bread cubes. Pour the hot vinegar mixture over, tossing to combine. Divide among 4 plates and serve warm.

Helpful hint: The grit will wash out of spinach more easily if you dunk the leaves in a basin of lukewarm, rather than cold, water.

FAT: 6G/16%
CALORIES: 347
SATURATED FAT: 1G
CARBOHYDRATE: 60G
PROTEIN: 16G
CHOLESTEROL: 11MG
SODIUM: 886MG

POTATO, HAM, AND CHEESE SALAD

SERVES: 4
WORKING TIME: 20 MINUTES
TOTAL TIME: 30 MINUTES

Tender asparagus lifts this simple salad out of the ordinary. But there's no extra fuss because the asparagus is cooked right along with the potatoes. The dressing is a versatile mustard vinaigrette that suits all sorts of salads. In fact, you might want to mix up an extra batch of the dressing and store it in the refrigerator for spur-of-the-moment use.

2 pounds red potatoes, quartered (or cut into eighths if large)

¾ pound asparagus, cut into 2-inch lengths

¼ cup balsamic or red wine vinegar

¼ cup reduced-sodium chicken broth, defatted

1 tablespoon Dijon mustard

2 teaspoons olive oil

½ teaspoon salt

1 red onion, finely chopped

1½ cups thawed frozen or no-salt-added canned corn kernels

3 ounces Cheddar cheese, cut into 1 x ¼-inch strips

3 ounces baked ham, in one piece, cut into 1 x ¼-inch strips

1. In a large pot of boiling water, cook the potatoes until tender, about 10 minutes. Add the asparagus for the last 2 minutes of cooking time to blanch. Drain.

2. Meanwhile, in a large bowl, combine the vinegar, broth, mustard, oil, and salt. Add the onion, stirring to combine. Add the potatoes and asparagus, tossing to coat.

3. Fold in the corn, Cheddar, and ham and serve warm, at room temperature, or chilled.

Helpful hint: The salad can be made up to 8 hours in advance; don't add the blanched asparagus until just before serving, otherwise, the vinegar in the dressing will cause the green vegetable to change color.

FAT: 12G/26%
CALORIES: 424
SATURATED FAT: 5.6G
CARBOHYDRATE: 61G
PROTEIN: 20G
CHOLESTEROL: 35MG
SODIUM: 876MG

HOPPIN' JOHN SALAD

SERVES: 4
WORKING TIME: 20 MINUTES
TOTAL TIME: 45 MINUTES

1½ cups reduced-sodium chicken broth, defatted

1 cup long-grain rice

½ teaspoon salt

10-ounce package frozen black-eyed peas

3 cloves garlic, minced

½ teaspoon dried sage

½ pound green beans, cut into 2-inch lengths

¼ cup red wine vinegar

4 teaspoons olive oil

2 teaspoons Dijon mustard

1 teaspoon hot pepper sauce

2 cups cherry tomatoes, halved

4 scallions, thinly sliced

3 ounces thinly sliced baked ham, slivered

4 cups watercress, tough stems removed

1. In a medium saucepan, bring the broth and 2 cups of water to a boil over medium heat. Add the rice and ¼ teaspoon of the salt, reduce to a simmer, cover, and cook for 5 minutes. Add the black-eyed peas, garlic, and sage; cover and cook until the rice and black-eyed peas are tender, about 22 minutes. Place the green beans on top of the rice mixture, cover, and cook until the green beans are crisp-tender, about 4 minutes.

2. Meanwhile, in a large bowl, combine the vinegar, oil, mustard, hot pepper sauce, and the remaining ¼ teaspoon salt. Stir in the rice mixture and fluff with a fork. Add the cherry tomatoes, scallions, and ham. Divide the watercress evenly among 4 plates, top with the rice mixture, and serve warm or at room temperature.

Helpful hint: Tart-bitter greens set this salad off to perfection. You could substitute chicory, escarole, or arugula for the watercress.

FAT: 7G/16%
CALORIES: 395
SATURATED FAT: 1.5G
CARBOHYDRATE: 64G
PROTEIN: 18G
CHOLESTEROL: 13MG
SODIUM: 927MG

A_s Southern folklore would have it, Hoppin' John—a dish of black-eyed peas and rice—brings good luck if eaten on New Year's Day. We hope that this interpretation of that classic dish will bring you good fortune, and we suspect you'll be enjoying it more than once a year. We've added tomatoes, watercress, mustard, and hot pepper sauce for color and a bit of a kick.

PASTA-CHEESE SALAD WITH SUN-DRIED TOMATOES

SERVES: 4
WORKING TIME: 20 MINUTES
TOTAL TIME: 30 MINUTES

The modernization of the macaroni salad required a change of pasta (to thimble-shaped ditalini), a nutritional boost (we added broccoli and raisins), and a flavor makeover (accomplished with sun-dried tomatoes, Parmesan, garlic, and fresh basil). The result is quite a spiffy update of good old macaroni with mayonnaise!

¼ cup (not oil-packed) sun-dried tomatoes
3 cloves garlic, peeled
10 ounces ditalini pasta
3 cups broccoli florets
⅔ cup part-skim ricotta cheese
⅓ cup low-fat (1%) cottage cheese
⅔ cup low-fat (1%) milk
¼ cup grated Parmesan cheese
2 teaspoons olive oil
½ teaspoon salt
¼ teaspoon freshly ground black pepper
½ cup raisins
⅓ cup chopped fresh basil
¼ cup coarsely chopped pecans

1. In a large pot of boiling water, cook the sun-dried tomatoes for about 5 minutes to soften. Add the garlic for the last 2 minutes of cooking. With a slotted spoon, remove the sun-dried tomatoes and garlic. When the sun-dried tomatoes are cool enough to handle, coarsely chop them.

2. Add the pasta to the boiling water and cook until just tender. Add the broccoli during the last 2 minutes of cooking time. Drain. Rinse under cold water, drain again.

3. In a food processor, combine the blanched garlic, ricotta, cottage cheese, milk, Parmesan, oil, salt, and pepper and process to a smooth purée. Transfer the purée to a large bowl, fold in the sun-dried tomatoes, raisins, basil, pecans, broccoli, and pasta. Divide among 4 plates and serve.

Helpful hint: This salad is best served warm or at room temperature; you can refrigerate it for an hour or so, but longer chilling will cause the dressing to thicken, changing the texture of the salad.

FAT: 14G/23%
CALORIES: 545
SATURATED FAT: 4.3G
CARBOHYDRATE: 83G
PROTEIN: 25G
CHOLESTEROL: 19MG
SODIUM: 569MG

TOMATO-MOZZARELLA SALAD WITH PESTO DRESSING

SERVES: 4
WORKING TIME: 15 MINUTES
TOTAL TIME: 25 MINUTES

The time to make this salad is when tasty vine-ripened tomatoes are available. Luckily, that's high season for fresh basil, too.

4 cloves garlic, peeled

8 ounces orzo pasta

1 cup packed fresh basil leaves

½ cup reduced-sodium chicken broth, defatted

⅓ cup grated Parmesan cheese

2 tablespoons reduced-fat cream cheese (Neufchâtel)

1 tablespoon reduced-fat mayonnaise

½ teaspoon salt

1½ pounds tomatoes, cut into ½-inch-wide wedges

4 cups mixed torn greens

1 cup shredded part-skim mozzarella cheese (4 ounces)

1. In a large pot of boiling water, cook the garlic for 2 minutes to blanch. With a slotted spoon, remove the garlic and set aside. Add the pasta to the boiling water and cook until just tender. Drain well.

2. In a food processor, combine the blanched garlic, basil, broth, Parmesan, cream cheese, mayonnaise, and salt and process to a smooth purée. Transfer the purée to a large bowl along with the pasta and tomatoes, tossing well to combine.

3. Divide the greens evenly among 4 plates, top with the pasta mixture, sprinkle the mozzarella over, and serve at room temperature or chilled.

Helpful hint: The salad can be made up to 1 hour in advance; don't place it on the greens or add the cheese until just before serving.

FAT: 11G/24%
CALORIES: 415
SATURATED FAT: 5.3G
CARBOHYDRATE: 61G
PROTEIN: 22G
CHOLESTEROL: 25MG
SODIUM: 694MG

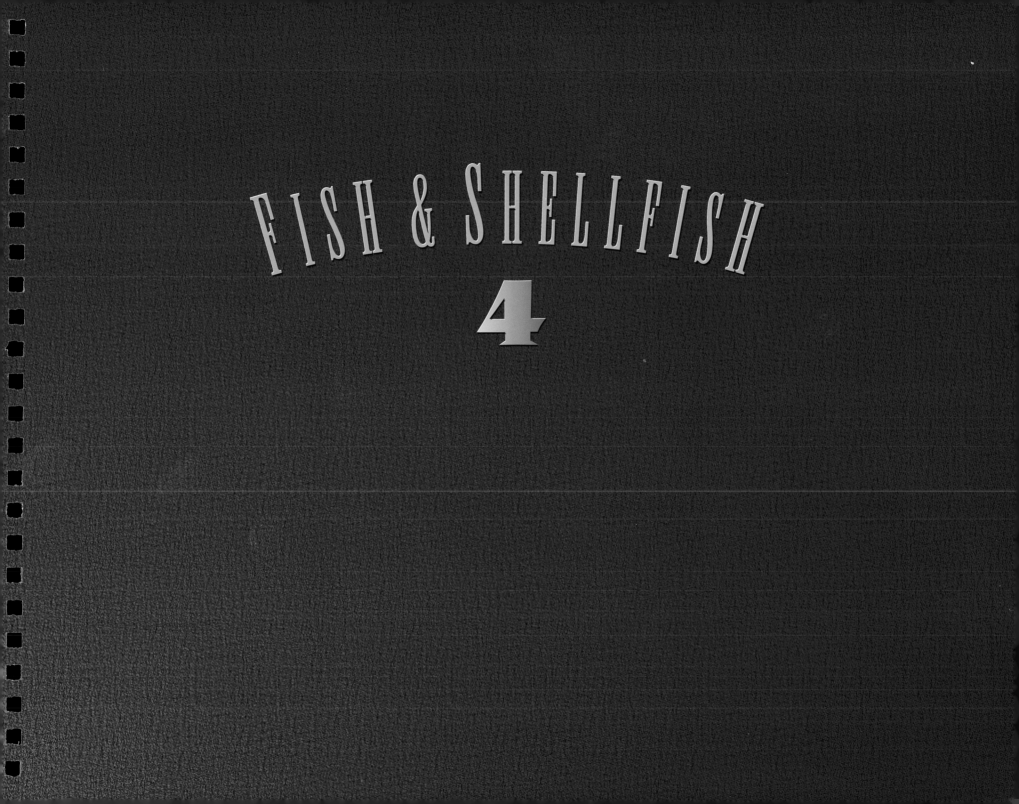

FISH & SHELLFISH
4

Shrimp are always a treat, and they cook in a flash. So they're just the thing for this quick meal that's sure to please everyone. To enhance their flavor, the shrimp are cooked in a garlic-flavored broth; using the broth in the dressing saves its goodness. The salad is seasoned with tarragon, an herb that is particularly effective with seafood.

ALL-AMERICAN SHRIMP SALAD

SERVES: 4
WORKING TIME: 20 MINUTES
TOTAL TIME: 25 MINUTES

1¼ pounds all-purpose potatoes, peeled and cut into ½-inch cubes

1 cup reduced-sodium chicken broth, defatted

2 cloves garlic, minced

1 pound medium shrimp, shelled and deveined (see tip)

¾ cup plain nonfat yogurt

3 tablespoons reduced-fat mayonnaise

2 tablespoons fresh lemon juice

½ teaspoon dried tarragon

½ teaspoon salt

¼ teaspoon freshly ground black pepper

3 scallions, thinly sliced

1 red bell pepper, cut into ½-inch squares

12 Boston lettuce leaves

12 green leaf lettuce leaves

1. In a large pot of boiling water, cook the potatoes until firm-tender, about 7 minutes. Drain.

2. Meanwhile, in a large skillet, bring the broth and garlic to a boil. Reduce to a simmer, add the shrimp, and cook until the shrimp are just opaque, about 4 minutes. Drain, reserving ⅓ cup of the cooking liquid. When cool enough to handle, halve the shrimp crosswise.

3. In a large bowl, combine the reserved cooking liquid, the yogurt, mayonnaise, lemon juice, tarragon, salt, and black pepper. Add the potatoes, shrimp, scallions, and bell pepper, stirring to coat. Divide the Boston and green leaf lettuce among 4 plates, spoon the shrimp mixture over, and serve warm, at room temperature, or chilled.

Helpful hints: The salad can be made up to 8 hours ahead; don't spoon it over the lettuce until just before serving. Feel free to use other lettuces for the Boston and green leaf: Bibb, romaine, iceberg, and red leaf would all work well.

FAT: 4G/14%
CALORIES: 260
SATURATED FAT: 0.8G
CARBOHYDRATE: 31G
PROTEIN: 25G
CHOLESTEROL: 141MG
SODIUM: 615MG

SALMON AND SUGAR SNAPS WITH DILL DRESSING

SERVES: 4
WORKING TIME: 20 MINUTES
TOTAL TIME: 30 MINUTES

Sugar snap peas—a cross between snow peas and regular green peas—have only been around since the 1970s, but they've certainly caught on. Plump and sweet, with a completely edible pod, sugar snaps are tasty raw, blanched, steamed, or stir-fried. You'll love them in this potato-and-salmon salad with a dilled mustard-lemon dressing; be sure to buy extra to munch while you're cooking.

1 pound red potatoes, cut into bite-size chunks

2 cups sugar snap peas, strings removed

10-ounce package frozen corn kernels

½ cup bottled clam juice, or reduced-sodium chicken broth, defatted

¾ pound salmon fillet

2 tablespoons reduced-fat mayonnaise

1 teaspoon grated lemon zest

2 tablespoons fresh lemon juice

1 tablespoon olive oil

1 tablespoon Dijon mustard

½ teaspoon salt

¼ teaspoon freshly ground black pepper

¼ cup snipped fresh dill

6 cups mixed torn greens

1. In a large pot of boiling water, cook the potatoes until just tender, about 12 minutes. Add the sugar snap peas and corn for the last 2 minutes of cooking time. Drain well.

2. Meanwhile, in a small skillet, bring the clam juice to a boil over medium heat. Add the salmon, return to a boil, cover, and cook until just opaque, 8 to 10 minutes. With a slotted spatula, transfer the salmon to a plate and set aside to cool. Reserve ⅓ cup of the cooking liquid. When cool enough to handle, discard the skin and cut the salmon into bite-size chunks.

3. In a large bowl, combine the reserved cooking liquid, the mayonnaise, lemon zest, lemon juice, oil, mustard, salt, and pepper, whisking to blend. Stir in the dill. Add the potatoes, sugar snap peas, and corn, tossing to coat with the dressing. Gently fold in the salmon. Divide the greens among 4 plates, spoon the salmon mixture over, and serve warm, at room temperature, or chilled.

Helpful hint: Mild-flavored green and red leaf lettuces would work well in this salad, as would a mix of escarole, endive, and radicchio.

FAT: 11G/26%
CALORIES: 386
SATURATED FAT: 1.7G
CARBOHYDRATE: 48G
PROTEIN: 25G
CHOLESTEROL: 47MG
SODIUM: 564MG

SWORDFISH AND ORANGE SALAD

SERVES: 4
WORKING TIME: 25 MINUTES
TOTAL TIME: 45 MINUTES

With its dense texture, swordfish can be treated in much the same way as meat— you don't have to coddle it the way you do more delicate fish. For this salad, swordfish steak is roasted with red potatoes—both coated with a rosemary-scented marinade. Oranges in the salad and orange juice in the dressing supply a brisk contrast to the rich flavor of the fish.

1 pound red potatoes, cut into bite-size pieces

2 tablespoons reduced-sodium chicken broth, defatted

2 tablespoons balsamic vinegar

2 teaspoons Dijon mustard

1 teaspoon paprika

1 teaspoon dried rosemary, crumbled

1 teaspoon salt

½ teaspoon freshly ground black pepper

1 pound swordfish steak

¼ cup orange juice

1 tablespoon olive oil

½ cup chopped scallions

2 tablespoons chopped Calamata or other brine-cured black olives

2 oranges, sectioned

6 cups mixed torn greens

1. In a large pot of boiling water, cook the potatoes until firm-tender, about 10 minutes.

2. Preheat the oven to 450°. Lightly spray a shallow roasting pan with nonstick cooking spray. In a small bowl, combine the broth, vinegar, mustard, paprika, rosemary, ½ teaspoon of the salt, and ¼ teaspoon of the pepper. Place the swordfish and cooked potatoes in the prepared pan and brush with the broth mixture. Roast, turning once, for 12 to 14 minutes, or until the swordfish is just opaque. Remove the pan from the oven and set aside to cool. When cool enough to handle, skin the swordfish and cut it into bite-size pieces.

3. Meanwhile, in a large bowl, combine the orange juice, oil, the remaining ½ teaspoon salt, and remaining ¼ teaspoon pepper. Stir in the scallions and olives. Add the roasted potatoes, swordfish, and orange sections, tossing gently to coat. Serve over the greens warm, at room temperature, or chilled.

Helpful hint: Depending on the fish's diet, swordfish flesh when raw can vary from pale beige to rosy pink; whatever its original shade, it will turn a cream color when cooked.

FAT: 10G/28%
CALORIES: 325
SATURATED FAT: 1.8G
CARBOHYDRATE: 36G
PROTEIN: 24G
CHOLESTEROL: 39MG
SODIUM: 814MG

Crab Louis originated on the West Coast. However opinions differ as to whether its birthplace was Seattle or San Francisco. At any rate, it's a wonderful way to showcase the luxury of lump crabmeat. We've lightened up the standard recipe, substituting nonfat yogurt for heavy cream and grapefruit sections for the traditional garnish of hard-cooked eggs.

CRAB LOUIS

SERVES: 4
WORKING TIME: 15 MINUTES
TOTAL TIME: 15 MINUTES

½ pound sugar snap peas, strings removed

½ cup plain nonfat yogurt

3 tablespoons chili sauce

1 tablespoon reduced-fat mayonnaise

1 tablespoon fresh lemon juice

½ teaspoon dried tarragon

¼ teaspoon salt

⅛ teaspoon cayenne pepper

1 pound lump crabmeat, picked over to remove any cartilage (see tip)

5 plum tomatoes, cut into 1-inch wedges

½ cup diced avocado

4 cups watercress, tough stems removed

3 grapefruits, peeled and sectioned

1. In a small pot of boiling water, cook the sugar snap peas for 30 seconds to blanch. Drain well.

2. In a large bowl, combine the yogurt, chili sauce, mayonnaise, lemon juice, tarragon, salt, and cayenne. Add the crabmeat, tomatoes, avocado, and sugar snap peas, tossing gently to combine.

3. Divide the watercress evenly among 4 plates. Arrange the grapefruit sections on top of the watercress, spoon the crab mixture over, and serve at room temperature or chilled.

Helpful hint: If fresh sugar snap peas are out of season, use frozen ones, if available. Or, substitute fresh or frozen snow peas.

FAT: 6G/19%
CALORIES: 284
SATURATED FAT: 0.9G
CARBOHYDRATE: 30G
PROTEIN: 29G
CHOLESTEROL: 114MG
SODIUM: 701MG

TIP

Lump crabmeat consists of large chunks of meat from the body (rather than the claws) of the crab. Before using lump crabmeat, whether fresh or canned, look it over carefully and remove any bits of cartilage or shell that may have remained in the meat. Don't over-handle the crabmeat or the "lumps" will fall apart.

Broiled Tuna and Pepper Salad

Serves: 4
Working time: 30 minutes
Total time: 35 minutes

¾ pound tuna steak

¼ cup reduced-sodium chicken broth, defatted

2 cloves garlic

½ cup low-sodium tomato-vegetable juice

2 tablespoons red wine vinegar

1 tablespoon olive oil

3 tablespoons chopped fresh basil

¾ teaspoon salt

½ teaspoon freshly ground black pepper

19-ounce can white kidney beans (cannellini), rinsed and drained

1 red bell pepper, diced

1 yellow bell pepper, diced

2 tomatoes, diced

1 cup sliced radishes

½ cup sliced scallions

1. Preheat the broiler. Brush the tuna with the broth. Broil the tuna 6 inches from the heat, turning once, for 5 minutes, or until just barely opaque. Set aside to cool, then cut into bite-size pieces.

2. In a small pot of boiling water, cook the garlic for 2 minutes to blanch. Drain and finely chop.

3. In a large bowl, combine the chopped garlic, tomato-vegetable juice, vinegar, oil, basil, salt, and black pepper. Stir in the kidney beans, bell peppers, tomatoes, radishes, and scallions, tossing to coat thoroughly. Gently fold in the tuna and serve warm, at room temperature, or chilled.

Helpful hint: Fresh tuna steak should look glossy and translucent and, like all seafood, have an ocean-fresh smell. Raw tuna is quite soft but firms up considerably when cooked.

Fat: 8g/26%
Calories: 280
Saturated Fat: 1.5g
Carbohydrate: 25g
Protein: 27g
Cholesterol: 29mg
Sodium: 682mg

There's a place for canned tuna, but fresh tuna—a dense, flavorful fish—is called for in this innovative salad featuring the popular fish, along with white kidney beans and crisp raw vegetables in a tomato-basil dressing. You could serve this salad on a lettuce-lined platter, or accompany it with a simple mix of leafy greens. Offer a basket of French or Italian rolls, as well.

Cod Salad with Parsley Dressing

SERVES: 4
WORKING TIME: 20 MINUTES
TOTAL TIME: 30 MINUTES

Cod, with its mild flavor, is a versatile salad ingredient. It's terrific with olives and capers in this Portuguese-inspired dish.

1 pound all-purpose potatoes, peeled and cut into ½-inch cubes

¾ cup bottled clam juice, or reduced-sodium chicken broth, defatted

1 pound cod fillet, any visible bones removed

3 cloves garlic

½ cup finely chopped fresh parsley

2 tablespoons white wine vinegar

1 tablespoon olive oil

1 tablespoon Dijon mustard

½ teaspoon salt

¼ teaspoon freshly ground black pepper

2 tablespoons capers, rinsed and drained

2 cups quartered cherry tomatoes

¼ cup Calamata or other brine-cured black olives, pitted and slivered

6 cups torn romaine lettuce

1. In a large pot of boiling water, cook the potatoes until firm-tender, about 12 minutes. Drain and transfer to a large bowl.

2. Meanwhile, in a medium skillet, bring the clam juice to a simmer, add the cod, cover and cook until the cod is just opaque, 9 to 10 minutes. Add the garlic cloves for the last 2 minutes of cooking time. With a slotted spatula, transfer the cod to a plate. Measure out ½ cup of the cooking liquid and transfer to a food processor or blender. Peel the garlic and add to the food processor.

3. Add the parsley, vinegar, oil, mustard, salt, pepper, and ¼ cup of the cooked potatoes to the food processor. Process to a smooth purée. Stir in the capers.

4. Break the cod into bite-size chunks and add to the potatoes in the bowl. Add the tomatoes, parsley dressing, and olives, tossing gently to combine. Divide the lettuce among 4 plates, spoon the cod mixture over, and serve warm, at room temperature, or chilled.

Helpful hint: You can substitute another lettuce such as iceberg, Boston, or Bibb for the romaine, if you like.

FAT: 7G/24%
CALORIES: 259
SATURATED FAT: 0.9G
CARBOHYDRATE: 25G
PROTEIN: 24G
CHOLESTEROL: 49MG
SODIUM: 773MG

Sweet and Tangy Fish Salad

SERVES: 4
WORKING TIME: 25 MINUTES
TOTAL TIME: 35 MINUTES

1 cup long-grain rice

1 teaspoon salt

½ cup bottled clam juice, or reduced-sodium chicken broth, defatted

1 pound red snapper fillets

1 clove garlic, peeled

1 teaspoon grated lime zest

¼ cup fresh lime juice

1 tablespoon honey

1 tablespoon olive oil

¼ teaspoon red pepper flakes

2 cups pineapple chunks, fresh or juice-packed canned

1 red bell pepper, diced

½ cup diced red onion

¼ cup golden or dark raisins

2 tablespoons chopped green olives

4 cups torn mixed greens

1. In a medium saucepan, bring 2¼ cups of water to a boil. Add the rice and ¼ teaspoon of the salt, reduce to a simmer, cover, and cook until the rice is tender, about 17 minutes.

2. Meanwhile, in a medium skillet, bring the clam juice to a boil over medium-high heat. Add the snapper, cover, and cook until just opaque, 6 to 7 minutes. Add the garlic for the last 1 minute of cooking time. With a slotted spatula, transfer the snapper to a plate. Remove the garlic and mince. Measure out ⅓ cup of the cooking liquid.

3. In a large bowl, combine the reserved cooking liquid, the chopped garlic, lime zest, lime juice, honey, oil, the remaining ¾ teaspoon salt, and the red pepper flakes. Stir in the pineapple, bell pepper, onion, raisins, and olives. Discard the snapper skin and with a fork, flake the snapper into bite-size pieces; gently fold the pieces into the salad along with the rice. Divide the greens among 4 plates, spoon the salad over, and serve warm, at room temperature, or chilled.

Helpful hints: Serve this salad shortly after it's made, or the rice will absorb the dressing and the salad will be dry. For a change, serve over a bed of fresh spinach.

FAT: 6G/13%
CALORIES: 428
SATURATED FAT: 1G
CARBOHYDRATE: 65G
PROTEIN: 29G
CHOLESTEROL: 42MG
SODIUM: 780MG

A tropical dressing made with lime juice, honey, and red pepper flakes adds excitement to this refreshing salad.

SPICY ITALIAN SHRIMP SALAD

SERVES: 4
WORKING TIME: 30 MINUTES
TOTAL TIME: 30 MINUTES

This pasta salad is made pretty much the same way as you would prepare a hot tomato-sauced pasta; however, the sauce is a real quickie rather than a recipe that requires all-day simmering. You can substitute another tube-shaped pasta for the ziti. Penne and elbow macaroni would both work well. Serve the salad with a hearty whole-grain Italian peasant loaf.

8 ounces ziti pasta

1 tablespoon olive oil

3 cloves garlic, minced

2 pickled jalapeños, finely chopped

1 pound medium shrimp, shelled and deveined

⅔ cup bottled clam juice, or reduced-sodium chicken broth, defatted

2 cups no-salt-added canned tomatoes, chopped with their juices

1 teaspoon dried tarragon

¾ teaspoon salt

1 teaspoon cornstarch mixed with 1 tablespoon water

3 ribs celery, halved lengthwise and thinly sliced

1 cucumber, peeled, halved lengthwise, seeded, and cut into ¼-inch dice

½ cup chopped fresh parsley

1. In a large pot of boiling water, cook the pasta until just tender. Drain well.

2. Meanwhile, in a large nonstick skillet, heat the oil until hot but not smoking over medium heat. Add the garlic and jalapeños and cook, stirring frequently, until the garlic is softened, about 3 minutes. Add the shrimp and cook, stirring frequently, until the shrimp are just opaque, about 3 minutes. With a slotted spoon, transfer the shrimp to a plate and when cool enough to handle, halve crosswise.

3. Add the clam juice to the skillet, increase the heat to high, and cook, stirring frequently, until reduced to ½ cup, about 3 minutes. Add the tomatoes, tarragon, and salt. Bring to a boil and cook for 2 minutes, stirring frequently. Add the cornstarch mixture and cook, stirring, until slightly thickened, about 1 minute.

4. Transfer the tomato mixture to a large bowl and add the pasta, shrimp, celery, cucumber, and parsley, tossing well. Serve warm, at room temperature, or chilled.

Helpful hint: For added Italian flavor, you can substitute 1 cup of chopped fresh fennel for the celery.

FAT: 6G/14%
CALORIES: 386
SATURATED FAT: 0.9G
CARBOHYDRATE: 54G
PROTEIN: 28G
CHOLESTEROL: 140MG
SODIUM: 797MG

ASIAN-STYLE SCALLOP SALAD

SERVES: 4
WORKING TIME: 15 MINUTES
TOTAL TIME: 35 MINUTES

Poached scallops in a nest of noodles retain their delicate flavor when bathed in a light Japanese-style dressing made with soy sauce, wine vinegar, and sesame oil. We've used vermicelli (very thin spaghetti) instead of Japanese noodles.

If you like to experiment, make the dish with Japanese soba, which are thin, buff-colored noodles made with buckwheat flour.

8 ounces vermicelli pasta

2 carrots, cut into 2 x ¼-inch julienne strips

1 red bell pepper, cut into 2-inch julienne strips

½ cup bottled clam juice, or reduced-sodium chicken broth, defatted

2 tablespoons minced fresh ginger

1 clove garlic, minced

1 pound sea scallops, halved

¼ cup reduced-sodium soy sauce

3 tablespoons white wine vinegar

1 tablespoon dark Oriental sesame oil

2 teaspoons Dijon mustard

8-ounce can sliced water chestnuts, drained

1 cup julienne-cut scallions

1 tablespoon sesame seeds, toasted

1. In a large pot of boiling water, cook the pasta until just tender. Add the carrots and bell pepper during the last 1 minute of cooking time. Drain well.

2. Meanwhile, in a medium saucepan, combine the clam juice, 1 tablespoon of the ginger, and the garlic. Bring to a boil over medium heat and add the scallops. Return to a boil and cook until the scallops are just opaque throughout, about 3 minutes. Drain, reserving ⅓ cup of the cooking liquid.

3. In a large bowl, combine the reserved cooking liquid, the soy sauce, vinegar, sesame oil, mustard, and the remaining 1 tablespoon ginger. Add the pasta, carrots, bell pepper, scallops, water chestnuts, and scallions, tossing to coat thoroughly. Divide the salad among 4 plates, sprinkle with the sesame seeds, and serve at room temperature or chilled.

Helpful hint: Toast the sesame seeds in a dry skillet over medium heat: Cook, stirring, for 2 to 3 minutes, until the seeds are golden brown.

FAT: 6G/13%
CALORIES: 416
SATURATED FAT: 0.9G
CARBOHYDRATE: 59G
PROTEIN: 29G
CHOLESTEROL: 38MG
SODIUM: 911MG

There's a summery seashore flavor to this pasta salad. The cod, shrimp, and scallops are cooked in a zesty broth of clam juice, lemon juice, and seasonings; and there's still more lemon (both juice and zest) in the peppery dressing. The vivid colors of asparagus, strips of yellow bell pepper, and slivers of red onion are laced throughout the linguine.

Seafood Salad with Lemon-Pepper Dressing

SERVES: 4
WORKING TIME: 25 MINUTES
TOTAL TIME: 30 MINUTES

8 ounces linguine

½ pound asparagus, trimmed and cut into 2-inch lengths

½ cup bottled clam juice, or reduced-sodium chicken broth, defatted

5 tablespoons fresh lemon juice

1 cup diced celery

1 tablespoon fennel seeds, crushed

2 cloves garlic, minced

½ teaspoon red pepper flakes

¼ pound medium shrimp, shelled, deveined, and halved lengthwise

¼ pound bay scallops (see tip)

½ pound cod fillet, cut into bite-size pieces

2 tablespoons olive oil

¾ teaspoon grated lemon zest

1 teaspoon salt

⅛ teaspoon freshly ground black pepper

1 yellow bell pepper, cut into thin strips

½ cup thinly sliced red onion

1. In a large pot of boiling water, cook the linguine until just tender. Add the asparagus during the last 2 minutes of cooking time. Drain well and set aside to cool.

2. Meanwhile, in a medium saucepan, combine the clam juice, 2 tablespoons of the lemon juice, the celery, fennel seeds, garlic, and ¼ teaspoon of the red pepper flakes. Bring to a boil over medium heat. Add the the shrimp, scallops, and cod; return to a boil, cover, and cook until the shrimp are just opaque, 3 to 4 minutes. Drain, reserving ⅓ cup of the cooking liquid.

3. In a large bowl, combine the reserved cooking liquid, the remaining 3 tablespoons lemon juice, the oil, lemon zest, salt, the remaining ¼ teaspoon red pepper flakes, and the black pepper. Add the linguine, asparagus, bell pepper, and onion, tossing to coat thoroughly. Gently fold in the shrimp, scallops, and cod. Divide among 4 plates and serve at room temperature or chilled.

Helpful hints: Use a mortar and pestle to crush whole fennel seeds. If you're fond of fresh fennel, substitute it for the celery; the fennel seeds will further accentuate its flavor.

FAT: 9G/20%
CALORIES: 408
SATURATED FAT: 1.2G
CARBOHYDRATE: 52G
PROTEIN: 30G
CHOLESTEROL: 70MG
SODIUM: 740MG

TIP

Tender, sweet bay scallops, no bigger across than a dime, may only be available seasonally. The larger sea scallops—about 1½ inches in diameter—are usually available year-round. If you can't find the smaller bay scallops, cut sea scallops into quarters to produce a reasonable facsimile.

SHRIMP CAESAR SALAD

SERVES: 4
WORKING TIME: 15 MINUTES
TOTAL TIME: 25 MINUTES

1 cup reduced-sodium chicken broth, defatted

1 pound medium shrimp, shelled and deveined

5 cloves garlic, peeled

3 tablespoons reduced-fat mayonnaise

¼ cup grated Parmesan cheese

½ teaspoon grated lemon zest

2 tablespoons fresh lemon juice

½ teaspoon salt

¼ teaspoon freshly ground black pepper

4 ounces Italian bread, halved horizontally

2 cups cherry tomatoes, halved

8 cups torn romaine or iceberg lettuce

1. In a large skillet, bring the broth to a boil over medium heat. Reduce to a simmer, add the shrimp, cover, and cook until the shrimp are just opaque, about 4 minutes. With a slotted spoon, transfer the shrimp to a plate. When cool enough to handle, halve the shrimp lengthwise.

2. Return the broth to a boil, add 4 of the garlic cloves, and cook for 2 minutes to blanch. Remove the garlic and reserve ¼ cup of the cooking liquid. In a food processor, combine the blanched garlic, the reserved cooking liquid, the mayonnaise, Parmesan, lemon zest, lemon juice, salt, and pepper and process to a smooth purée, about 1 minute. Transfer to a large bowl.

3. Preheat the broiler. Toast the bread 6 inches from the heat for about 1 minute per side, or until lightly browned. Rub the bread with the remaining clove of garlic, then cut the bread into ½-inch chunks. Add the bread to the dressing, along with the shrimp, tomatoes, and lettuce, tossing to combine. Divide the salad among 4 plates and serve at room temperature or chilled.

Helpful hint: We leave the tails on the shrimp for a prettier presentation, but if you prefer, you can remove the tails when shelling the shrimp.

FAT: 7G/24%
CALORIES: 264
SATURATED FAT: 1.9G
CARBOHYDRATE: 24G
PROTEIN: 26G
CHOLESTEROL: 144MG
SODIUM: 807MG

The basic Caesar salad, created in the 1920s, has enjoyed a recent renaissance. These days, it often moves up to main-dish status when grilled chicken is added. We think plump shrimp make it an even more appealing dish. Furthermore, our eggless dressing and toasted (not fried) croutons render it a healthier meal.

Spicy Tuna-Pasta Salad

SERVES: 4
WORKING TIME: 20 MINUTES
TOTAL TIME: 20 MINUTES

*I*nstead of a tuna sandwich, enjoy this lemony tuna-and-orzo salad with unexpected hints of hot pepper and cumin.

8 ounces orzo pasta
⅔ cup plain nonfat yogurt
¼ cup reduced-fat sour cream
2 tablespoons reduced-fat mayonnaise
1 teaspoon grated lemon zest
3 tablespoons fresh lemon juice
½ teaspoon hot pepper sauce
½ teaspoon salt
1 teaspoon ground cumin
Two 6½-ounce cans water-packed tuna, drained and flaked
1 cup diced celery
½ cup chopped scallions
¼ cup chopped fresh cilantro or parsley
6 cups mixed torn greens
4 tomatoes, cut into wedges
¼ cup diced avocado

1. In a large pot of boiling water, cook the pasta until just tender. Drain well.

2. Meanwhile, in a large bowl, combine the yogurt, sour cream, mayonnaise, lemon zest, lemon juice, hot pepper sauce, salt, and cumin, whisking to blend. Stir in the pasta, tuna, celery, scallions, and cilantro.

3. Arrange the greens and tomatoes on 4 plates, top with the tuna mixture, sprinkle with the avocado, and serve at room temperature or chilled.

Helpful hints: The salad can be made up to 8 hours in advance; don't spoon it over the greens or add the tomato and avocado until serving time. Read labels carefully when buying canned tuna: Some national brands of water-packed solid white tuna have as much as 5 grams of fat in 2 ounces. Look for a brand with no more than 1 gram of fat in 2 ounces.

FAT: 7G/14%
CALORIES: 454
SATURATED FAT: 1.9G
CARBOHYDRATE: 60G
PROTEIN: 38G
CHOLESTEROL: 40MG
SODIUM: 731MG

GRILLED SHRIMP AND SPRING VEGETABLE SALAD

SERVES: 4
WORKING TIME: 30 MINUTES
TOTAL TIME: 30 MINUTES

Chopped vegetables—bell peppers, scallion, and cucumber—make a colorful bed for a bounty of grilled shrimp. The shrimp are coated with an assertive spice rub before they go on the fire, and the same mixture of cumin, coriander, oregano, salt, and pepper seasons the dressing for the vegetable mixture. The salad is served over "Texas toast"—slices of grilled bread.

1 teaspoon ground cumin

1 teaspoon ground coriander

1 teaspoon dried oregano

¼ teaspoon salt

¼ teaspoon freshly ground black pepper

1 pound medium shrimp, shelled and deveined

1 red bell pepper, cut into 1-inch pieces

1 green bell pepper, cut into 1-inch pieces

1 scallion, cut into 1-inch lengths

½ cucumber, peeled, halved lengthwise, seeded, and cut into 1-inch pieces

⅔ cup low-sodium tomato-vegetable juice

1 tablespoon no-salt-added tomato paste

1 tablespoon white wine vinegar

1 tablespoon olive oil

4 ounces French bread, cut into ½-inch slices

1. In a medium bowl, combine the cumin, coriander, oregano, salt, and black pepper. Measure ¾ teaspoon of the spice mixture and set aside. Add the shrimp to the spices remaining in the bowl, tossing to combine. Let stand at room temperature for 10 minutes.

2. Meanwhile, in a food processor, combine the reserved ¾ teaspoon spice mixture, the bell peppers, scallion, cucumber, tomato-vegetable juice, tomato paste, vinegar, and oil. Process with on/off pulses until the vegetables are coarsely chopped. (Do this in batches if necessary.)

3. Preheat the grill. Thread the shrimp on skewers. Spray the rack—off the grill—with nonstick cooking spray. Place the skewers on the rack, cover, and grill at medium, or 6 inches from the heat, turning once, for 6 minutes, or until the shrimp are just opaque. Meanwhile, grill the bread, turning several times, for 4 minutes, or until lightly toasted.

4. Arrange the bread slices on 4 plates. Top with the shrimp, spoon the vegetable mixture over, and serve warm or at room temperature.

Helpful hints: You can cut up the vegetables by hand up to 4 hours in advance; to keep them from becoming soft, don't chop them in the food processor until close to serving time. You can measure out the spice mixture ahead of time as well.

FAT: 6G/23%
CALORIES: 237
SATURATED FAT: 0.9G
CARBOHYDRATE: 22G
PROTEIN: 22G
CHOLESTEROL: 140MG
SODIUM: 479MG

119

*S*ummer *is serious grilling season for people who live in northern climes, but it's worth firing up the grill in the fall to enjoy this autumnal meal. The pork tenderloin, sweet potato wedges, and pineapple slices are basted with gingery honey mustard as they cook; after grilling, they're tossed in a spicy pineapple-lime dressing.*

GRILLED PORK SALAD WITH HONEY MUSTARD

SERVES: 4
WORKING TIME: 20 MINUTES
TOTAL TIME: 40 MINUTES

1½ pounds sweet potatoes, peeled and halved lengthwise

3 tablespoons honey

3 tablespoons Dijon mustard

2 tablespoons grated fresh ginger

2 tablespoons reduced-sodium chicken broth, defatted

¼ teaspoon freshly ground black pepper

1 pound well-trimmed pork tenderloin

8 juice-packed canned pineapple slices, juice reserved

8 scallions

2 tablespoons cider vinegar

1 teaspoon grated lime zest

½ teaspoon salt

¼ teaspoon ground allspice

6 cups mesclun or mixed torn greens

1. In a large pot of boiling water, cook the sweet potatoes until firm-tender, about 12 minutes. Drain well.

2. Meanwhile, in a large bowl, combine the honey, mustard, ginger, broth, and pepper. Measure out ¼ cup of the mixture to use as a baste. Set the remainder in the large bowl aside.

3. Preheat the grill (with a grill topper, if possible; see tip). Spray the rack (or grill topper)—off the grill—with nonstick cooking spray. Place the sweet potatoes, pork, and pineapple on the grill. Cover and grill at high, or 4 inches from the heat, turning once and brushing with the honey-mustard baste, for 15 minutes, or until the pork is cooked through but still juicy and the sweet potatoes are tender. Add the scallions to the grill during the last 5 minutes of cooking time. Place the pork on a plate and let it stand for 10 minutes. When cool enough to handle, cut the sweet potatoes and pineapple into bite-size chunks. Cut the scallions into 1-inch lengths. Cut the pork into thin slices, reserving any juices on the plate.

4. Meanwhile, add ⅓ cup of the reserved pineapple juice, the vinegar, lime zest, salt, allspice, and pork juices to the honey-mustard mixture in the large bowl. Add the pork, sweet potatoes, pineapple, and scallions, tossing to coat. Line a platter with the mesclun, top with the salad, and serve warm or at room temperature.

FAT: 5G/11%
CALORIES: 404
SATURATED FAT: 1.5G
CARBOHYDRATE: 67G
PROTEIN: 24G
CHOLESTEROL: 60MG
SODIUM: 637MG

TIP

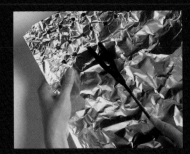

To make your own grill topper, tear off a large piece of heavy-duty foil and fold it in half to make a double layer. Using a two-tined fork, make a series of holes over the entire surface of the foil. Use the punctured foil to cover the grill rack—before preheating—and proceed as directed.

CAJUN CHICKEN SALAD

SERVES: 4
WORKING TIME: 25 MINUTES
TOTAL TIME: 35 MINUTES

In the past few years the term "blackened" has become a code word for "Cajun." But you don't have to grill chicken until it's scorched to create a Cajun-style meal. The peppery spice rub that goes under the chicken skin here is delicious and in fact, more authentically Cajun than blackening. The skin is discarded after grilling, so the fat disappears while the flavor remains.

1 pound red potatoes, cut into
  bite-size pieces
½ pound sugar snap peas, strings
  removed
2 cloves garlic, peeled
2 teaspoons paprika
1½ teaspoons dried oregano
1½ teaspoons dried thyme
1 teaspoon salt
½ teaspoon freshly ground black
  pepper
⅛ teaspoon cayenne pepper
1 pound boneless chicken breasts,
  with skin
⅓ cup reduced-sodium chicken
  broth, defatted
2 tablespoons red wine vinegar
1 tablespoon olive oil
2 teaspoons Dijon mustard
4 cups finely shredded red
  cabbage

1. In a large pot of boiling water, cook the potatoes until firm-tender, about 10 minutes. Add the sugar snap peas and garlic for the last 1 minute of cooking time. Drain. Finely chop the garlic and place in a large bowl.

2. Meanwhile, in a small bowl, combine the paprika, oregano, thyme, ½ teaspoon of the salt, the black pepper, and cayenne. Measure out 2 teaspoons of the spice mixture and add to the bowl with the garlic. Lift the skin of the chicken and rub the remaining 4 teaspoons spice mixture into the flesh.

3. Preheat the grill. Spray the rack—off the grill—with nonstick cooking spray. Place the chicken, skin-side up, on the grill rack. Cover and grill at medium, or 6 inches from the heat, turning once, for 8 to 10 minutes, or until the chicken is cooked through. When the chicken is cool enough to handle, remove and discard the skin and cut the breasts across the grain into thin slices.

4. Add the broth, vinegar, oil, mustard, and the remaining ½ teaspoon salt to the garlic and spices in the large bowl, whisking to combine. Add the potatoes, sugar snap peas, cabbage, and sliced chicken, tossing to coat. Divide among 4 plates and serve warm or at room temperature.

Helpful hint: You can substitute snow peas for the sugar snaps, if you like.

FAT: 7G/20%
CALORIES: 315
SATURATED FAT: 1.4G
CARBOHYDRATE: 32G
PROTEIN: 31G
CHOLESTEROL: 70MG
SODIUM: 740MG

NORTH CAROLINA BARBECUED CHICKEN SALAD

SERVES: 4
WORKING TIME: 25 MINUTES
TOTAL TIME: 40 MINUTES

2 cups shredded carrots

2 cups shredded parsnips or carrots

1 cup frozen corn kernels

2 tablespoons firmly packed light brown sugar

2 cloves garlic, minced

2 teaspoons paprika

1 teaspoon dry mustard

½ teaspoon ground ginger

¼ teaspoon cayenne pepper

1 teaspoon salt

2 tablespoons rice vinegar

¾ cup apple juice

1 tablespoon ketchup

1 tablespoon olive oil

1½ pounds bone-in chicken breasts, with skin

2 scallions, slivered

2 tablespoons chopped pecans

1. In a large pot of boiling water, cook the carrots, parsnips, and corn until the carrots are crisp-tender, about 5 minutes. Drain well.

2. Meanwhile, in a small bowl, combine the brown sugar, garlic, paprika, mustard, ginger, cayenne, and ¼ teaspoon of the salt. In a large bowl, combine 1½ tablespoons of the brown sugar mixture, the vinegar, apple juice, ketchup, oil, and the remaining ¾ teaspoon salt. Set the dressing aside.

3. Preheat the grill. Using your fingers, gently separate the skin from the chicken meat, leaving one side attached. Sprinkle the remaining brown sugar mixture over the chicken flesh and replace the skin. Place the chicken on the grill, skin-side up. Cover and grill at medium, or 6 inches from the heat, turning the chicken every 6 minutes, for 18 minutes, or until the chicken is cooked through. When the chicken is cool enough to handle, remove and discard the skin and shred the meat with your fingers.

4. Add the shredded chicken to the bowl of dressing along with the carrots, parsnips, corn, and scallions, tossing to combine. Divide among 4 plates, sprinkle the pecans over, and serve warm or at room temperature.

Helpful hint: To shred the chicken, first remove it from the bones; then, following the direction of the grain, pull the meat into strips.

FAT: 10G/25%
CALORIES: 359
SATURATED FAT: 1.5G
CARBOHYDRATE: 42G
PROTEIN: 29G
CHOLESTEROL: 69MG
SODIUM: 688MG

Across the South, barbecue fans strive to define "real" barbecue. In North Carolina, traditionalists mop the slow-cooked meat with a peppery vinegar sauce and serve it with cole slaw. Our sauce is made with some novel ingredients, including rice vinegar and apple juice, and we've fashioned a special slaw from carrots and parsnips. Corn bread would be an excellent accompaniment.

Beef and chili peppers are two indispensable ingredients in any Texas barbecue. In place of brisket—tender, but one of the fattiest of all beef cuts—we've used top round, which will be tender and juicy, too, if you baste it well and don't overcook it. Chili sauce serves as the "hot stuff" in the barbecue sauce. Serve the salad with sourdough rolls.

Texas Barbecued Beef Salad

SERVES: 4
WORKING TIME: 20 MINUTES
TOTAL TIME: 35 MINUTES

⅔ cup chili sauce

3 tablespoons firmly packed light
brown sugar

3 tablespoons cider vinegar

1½ teaspoons ground cumin

1 teaspoon ground coriander

3 tablespoons reduced-sodium
chicken broth, defatted

1 tablespoon olive oil

2 teaspoons Dijon mustard

¼ teaspoon salt

1 pound red potatoes, cut into
½-inch-thick slices

½ pound green beans, cut into
2-inch lengths

¾ pound well-trimmed top
round of beef

1 red onion, cut into
¼-inch-thick slices

6 cups mixed torn greens

1. In a medium bowl, combine the chili sauce, brown sugar, vinegar, cumin, and coriander. Measure out ⅓ cup of the chili sauce mixture to use as a baste. Add the broth, oil, mustard, and salt to the mixture remaining in the bowl. Set the dressing aside.

2. In a large pot of boiling water, cook the potatoes until almost tender, about 5 minutes. Drain well. In a separate pot of boiling water, cook the green beans until crisp-tender, about 3 minutes. Drain the beans and transfer to the bowl with the dressing.

3. Preheat the grill. Spray the rack—off the grill—with nonstick cooking spray. Place the cooked potatoes, beef, and onion on the grill. Cover and grill at medium, or 6 inches from the heat, turning once and basting with the reserved basting mixture, for 14 to 15 minutes, or until the beef is medium-rare and the vegetables are tender. When the beef is cool enough to handle, thinly slice it (see tip).

4. Add the beef, potatoes, and onions to the dressing, tossing to coat thoroughly. Line a platter with the greens, top with the salad, and serve warm or at room temperature.

Helpful hints: To speed things up at dinner time, you can prepare the chili sauce mixture up to 8 hours in advance and refrigerate it in a covered bowl or jar. Serve the salad over romaine, red leaf, or iceberg lettuce, or a combination of all three.

FAT: 7G/17%
CALORIES: 373
SATURATED FAT: 1.4G
CARBOHYDRATE: 53G
PROTEIN: 26G
CHOLESTEROL: 49MG
SODIUM: 909MG

T I P

Slice top round, flank steak, and other lean steaks into thin slices so that the meat will be as tender as possible.

GRILLED SPRING SALAD

SERVES: 4
WORKING TIME: 20 MINUTES
TOTAL TIME: 35 MINUTES

The cooling flavor of mint and the crunch of fresh radishes enliven this unusual salad of lamb, potatoes, and asparagus.

⅓ cup apple juice

¼ teaspoon hot pepper sauce

1 tablespoon olive oil

¼ cup chopped fresh mint

¼ cup cider vinegar

1 teaspoon salt

3 cloves garlic, minced

2 teaspoons ground cumin

2 teaspoons ground paprika

¾ pound well-trimmed leg of lamb, cut into 1-inch cubes

1 pound red potatoes, cut into ¾-inch pieces

¾ pound asparagus, tough ends trimmed and cut into 2-inch pieces

1 cup thinly sliced radishes

2 cups mixed torn greens

1. In a large bowl, combine the apple juice, hot pepper sauce, olive oil, 1 tablespoon of the mint, 1 tablespoon of the vinegar, and ¾ teaspoon of the salt. Set the dressing aside. In a medium bowl, combine the remaining 3 tablespoons mint, remaining 3 tablespoons vinegar, the garlic, cumin, paprika, and the remaining ¼ teaspoon salt. Add the lamb, tossing to coat. Let stand at room temperature for 15 minutes.

2. Meanwhile, in a large pot of boiling water, cook the potatoes until firm-tender, about 11 minutes. Add the asparagus for the last 6 minutes of cooking time. Drain well.

3. Preheat the grill. Thread the lamb on skewers. Spray the rack—off the grill—with nonstick cooking spray. Place the skewers on the rack, cover, and grill at medium, or 6 inches from the heat, turning once, for 6 to 8 minutes, or until the lamb is medium-rare.

4. Add the potatoes, asparagus, grilled lamb, and radishes to the dressing in the large bowl, tossing to coat thoroughly. Divide the greens among 4 plates, top with the salad, and serve warm or at room temperature.

Helpful hint: A mixture of red leaf and Boston lettuces would work well in this salad.

FAT: 9G/28%
CALORIES: 291
SATURATED FAT: 2.3G
CARBOHYDRATE: 30G
PROTEIN: 23G
CHOLESTEROL: 57MG
SODIUM: 624MG

GRILLED SWORDFISH AND LENTIL SALAD

SERVES: 4
WORKING TIME: 40 MINUTES
TOTAL TIME: 45 MINUTES

¾ cup lentils, rinsed and picked over

1 teaspoon dried tarragon

2 red bell peppers, 1 seeded and halved lengthwise, 1 diced

3 tablespoons fresh lemon juice

1 tablespoon honey

1½ teaspoons chili powder

¾ teaspoon salt

1½ pounds swordfish steaks

1 tomato, halved crosswise

2 tablespoons white wine vinegar

1½ teaspoons olive oil

¼ cup coarsely chopped chives or scallion greens

4 cups mixed torn greens

1. In a medium saucepan, combine 2 cups of water, the lentils, and ½ teaspoon of the tarragon and bring to a simmer. Cover and cook until tender, about 35 minutes. Drain and transfer to a medium bowl. Stir in the diced bell pepper.

2. Meanwhile, in a glass baking dish, combine the lemon juice, honey, chili powder, ¼ teaspoon of the salt, and the remaining ½ teaspoon tarragon. Add the swordfish, turning to coat. Let stand at room temperature for 15 minutes, turning occasionally.

3. Preheat the grill. Spray the rack—off the grill—with nonstick cooking spray. Place the swordfish, tomato, and bell pepper halves on the rack. Cover and grill at medium, or 6 inches from the heat, turning once and brushing the swordfish with any remaining marinade, for 10 minutes, or until the swordfish is just opaque and the vegetables are tender. When cool enough to handle, cut the swordfish into slices. Peel the tomato and cut the bell pepper into quarters.

4. In a food processor or blender, combine the bell pepper quarters, tomato, vinegar, oil, the remaining ½ teaspoon salt, and the chives and process to a smooth purée. Pour half of the dressing over the lentils, tossing to combine. Divide the greens among 4 plates, and top with the lentils. Place the swordfish alongside, drizzle the remaining dressing over, and serve.

FAT: 9G/21%
CALORIES: 388
SATURATED FAT: 2G
CARBOHYDRATE: 36G
PROTEIN: 43G
CHOLESTEROL: 59MG
SODIUM: 609MG

This sturdy lentil salad with honey-lemon-basted swordfish makes a light but extremely satisfying meal.

MARGARITA SCALLOP SALAD

SERVES: 4
WORKING TIME: 25 MINUTES
TOTAL TIME: 30 MINUTES

The margarita inspiration for this salad can be found in the dressing for the vegetables, which is made with orange juice, tequila, and lime juice. The plump sea scallops are also flavored with lime, as well as fresh herbs. Serve a basket of corn or flour tortillas with this Mexican-inspired meal: Heat the tortillas on the grill, then wrap them in a cloth napkin to keep them warm.

3 tablespoons fresh lime juice
2 tablespoons minced fresh parsley
1 teaspoon dried basil
1 pound sea scallops
¼ cup reduced-sodium chicken broth, defatted
2 tablespoons olive oil
¼ cup orange juice
1 tablespoon tequila
¼ teaspoon salt
¼ teaspoon freshly ground black pepper
1½ cups cherry tomatoes, halved
½ sweet onion, halved and thinly sliced
1 cup thinly sliced cucumber
1½ cups frozen corn kernels, thawed
2 cups mesclun or mixed torn greens

1. In a medium bowl, combine 2 tablespoons of the lime juice, the parsley, and basil. Add the scallops, tossing to coat. Let stand at room temperature for 10 minutes.

2. Meanwhile, in a large bowl, combine the broth, oil, orange juice, tequila, salt, pepper, and the remaining 1 tablespoon lime juice. Add the tomatoes, onion, cucumber, and corn, tossing to coat.

3. Preheat the grill. Thread the scallops on 8 skewers. Spray the rack—off the grill—with nonstick cooking spray. Place the skewers on the rack, cover, and grill at medium, or 6 inches from the heat, turning once, for 4 to 6 minutes, or until the scallops are just opaque throughout.

4. Place the mesclun on a platter and top with the tomato mixture and the scallops and serve warm or at room temperature.

Helpful hint: If you don't have any tequila on hand, try this with a white rum. Or, for an alcohol-free dish, simply leave out the tequila.

FAT: 8G/28%
CALORIES: 260
SATURATED FAT: 1.1G
CARBOHYDRATE: 24G
PROTEIN: 23G
CHOLESTEROL: 38MG
SODIUM: 366MG

Jamaican Jerk Chicken Salad

SERVES: 4
WORKING TIME: 25 MINUTES
TOTAL TIME: 35 MINUTES

The sweet spiciness of Jamaican jerk seasoning just begs to be paired with fruit. So we've come up with a grilled chicken salad that features mango and watermelon, along with grilled bell peppers. This is a magnificent dish as it is, but you might also like to serve the salad on a bed of sturdy deep-green lettuces.

4 scallions, cut into 1-inch lengths

2 tablespoons firmly packed light brown sugar

2 tablespoons ketchup

2 teaspoons paprika

2 teaspoons ground ginger

¼ teaspoon ground allspice

2 tablespoons red wine vinegar

2 tablespoons fresh lemon juice

1 tablespoon olive oil

½ teaspoon salt

¾ pound skinless, boneless chicken breasts, lightly pounded

2 green bell peppers, seeded and halved lengthwise

1 mango, pitted, peeled, and cut into 3-inch strips

2 cups seeded watermelon cubes (¾ inch)

1. In a mini-processor or blender, combine the scallions, brown sugar, ketchup, paprika, ginger, allspice, and vinegar and process until smooth. Measure out ¼ cup of the mixture to use as a baste. Transfer the remaining mixture to a large bowl and add the lemon juice, oil, and salt. Set the dressing aside.

2. Preheat the grill. Spray the rack—off the grill—with nonstick cooking spray. Rub the reserved basting mixture over the chicken. Place the chicken and bell pepper halves on the rack, cover, and grill at medium, or 6 inches from the heat, turning once, for 8 to 10 minutes, or until the chicken is cooked through.

3. Cut the grilled chicken and peppers into strips. Add to the bowl with the dressing, along with the mango and watermelon, tossing to combine. Divide among 4 plates and serve warm or at room temperature.

Helpful hint: If watermelon isn't available, you can substitute pineapple or cantaloupe.

FAT: 5G/19%
CALORIES: 241
SATURATED FAT: 0.8G
CARBOHYDRATE: 29G
PROTEIN: 21G
CHOLESTEROL: 49MG
SODIUM: 427MG

Garlic *is a multi-purpose ingredient in this salad. Of course, it contributes its popular pungent flavor (tempered somewhat by roasting on the grill), but it also serves to thicken the dressing in place of higher-fat ingredients. The basil-garlic vinaigrette coats a medley of radiatore pasta, squash, bell pepper, eggplant, tomatoes, and green olives.*

Pasta-Vegetable Salad with Garlic Dressing

SERVES: 4
WORKING TIME: 40 MINUTES
TOTAL TIME: 40 MINUTES

8 ounces radiatore pasta

9-ounce package frozen artichoke hearts, thawed

6 cloves garlic

¾ cup reduced-sodium chicken broth, defatted

3 tablespoons red wine vinegar

2 scallions, cut into 1-inch lengths

¼ cup chopped fresh basil

1½ tablespoons olive oil

¾ teaspoon salt

2 yellow summer squash, halved lengthwise

1 green bell pepper, seeded and halved lengthwise

1 eggplant (1 pound), peeled and cut lengthwise into ¾-inch pieces

8 plum tomatoes (1 pound total), halved lengthwise

¼ cup chopped pitted green olives

1 ounce shaved Parmesan, or ¼ cup grated Parmesan cheese

1. In a large pot of boiling water, cook the pasta until just tender. Add the artichokes for the last 6 minutes of cooking time. Drain and rinse under cold running water. Place in a large bowl.

2. Meanwhile, preheat the grill (with a grill topper, if possible). Wrap the garlic in foil. In a small bowl, combine the broth and vinegar. Set aside ¼ cup of the broth mixture to use as a baste. Place the remaining broth mixture in a food processor or blender along with the scallions, basil, oil, and salt; set the mixture aside in the processor bowl (or blender container).

3. Spray the rack (or grill topper)—off the grill—with nonstick cooking spray. Place the garlic, squash, bell pepper, and eggplant on the grill. Cover and grill at medium, or 6 inches from the heat, turning occasionally and basting with the reserved basting mixture, for 12 to 14 minutes, or until the vegetables are tender but not falling apart. Place the tomatoes (skin-sides down) on the grill for the last 6 minutes of cooking time.

4. Cut the vegetables into bite-size pieces and add to the bowl with the pasta and artichokes. Squeeze the garlic flesh from the grilled garlic cloves (see tip), add them to the food processor, and process the dressing to a smooth purée. Add the dressing and the olives to the bowl, tossing to coat. Divide among 4 plates, top with the Parmesan, and serve warm or at room temperature.

FAT: 10G/23%
CALORIES: 396
SATURATED FAT: 2G
CARBOHYDRATE: 66G
PROTEIN: 15G
CHOLESTEROL: 4MG
SODIUM: 866MG

TIP

Unwrap the grilled garlic cloves, then snip off the tip of each clove and squeeze out the roasted garlic, discarding the skin.

SALMON SALAD WITH ORANGE-DILL SAUCE

SERVES: 4
WORKING TIME: 20 MINUTES
TOTAL TIME: 45 MINUTES

½ cup orange juice

1½ tablespoons honey

1 tablespoon Dijon mustard

2 tablespoons snipped fresh dill

¼ teaspoon freshly ground black pepper

¾ pound salmon fillet

2 tablespoons chopped shallots or scallion whites

1 teaspoon olive oil

¼ teaspoon salt

2 zucchini, cut lengthwise into ½-inch-thick slabs

1 yellow summer squash, cut lengthwise into ½-inch-thick slabs

3 cups watercress, tough stems removed, very coarsely chopped

1¼ cups halved cherry tomatoes

1. In a small bowl, combine the orange juice, honey, mustard, dill, and pepper. Transfer ¼ cup of the mixture to a glass baking dish or large shallow bowl and add the salmon, turning to coat. Let stand at room temperature for 15 minutes, turning occasionally. Add the shallots, oil, and salt to the orange juice mixture remaining in the small bowl. Set the dressing aside.

2. Preheat the grill. Spray the rack—off the grill—with nonstick cooking spray. Reserving the marinade, place the salmon on the grill along with the zucchini and yellow squash. Brush the vegetables with some of the reserved marinade. Cover and grill at medium, or 6 inches from the heat, turning once and brushing the salmon and squash with more of the marinade, for 16 minutes, or until the salmon is just opaque and the vegetables are tender. When cool enough to handle, cut the zucchini and yellow squash into ¾-inch lengths. Remove and discard the salmon skin and break the fish into bite-size chunks.

3. In a medium bowl, toss the watercress and tomatoes with half of the dressing. Divide the watercress and tomatoes among 4 plates. Top with the zucchini, yellow squash, and salmon. Drizzle the remaining dressing over and serve warm or at room temperature.

Helpful hint: Another tart or bitter green, such as arugula, curly endive, or radicchio, could be substituted for the watercress.

FAT: 6G/27%
CALORIES: 197
SATURATED FAT: 1G
CARBOHYDRATE: 17G
PROTEIN: 18G
CHOLESTEROL: 43MG
SODIUM: 278MG

136

Salmon can be an elegant or casual dish, depending on how it's prepared. This tempting salad, with its lush chunks of citrus-grilled salmon, is versatile enough to serve either as a company meal or a weekday supper. It's a good idea to use a grill topper when cooking fish and cut-up vegetables; if you don't have one, you can improvise with a sheet of foil (see page 121).

For a meatless dish, this "mixed grill" has more than its share of meaty savor. The portobello mushrooms, bell peppers, and red onion develop a deliciously rich, smoky flavor on the grill, underscored by an herbed balsamic vinaigrette. As an alternative to grilling the mushrooms and onions on skewers, you could spread them on a grill topper.

Grilled Mushroom Salad

SERVES: 4
WORKING TIME: 25 MINUTES
TOTAL TIME: 35 MINUTES

3 tablespoons balsamic vinegar

2 tablespoons dry sherry

1 teaspoon dried sage

1 teaspoon dried thyme

1 pound portobello or very large button mushrooms, cut into 1-inch-wide slices

1 red onion, cut into 8 wedges

1 red bell pepper, seeded and halved lengthwise

1 green bell pepper, seeded and halved lengthwise

5 ounces French bread, cut into ½-inch slices

1 clove garlic, peeled and halved

¼ cup apple juice

2 teaspoons olive oil

¼ teaspoon hot pepper sauce

½ teaspoon salt

¼ cup plus 2 tablespoons shredded jalapeño jack cheese (1½ ounces)

1. In a medium bowl, combine the vinegar, sherry, sage, and thyme. Transfer 2 tablespoons to a large bowl and set aside. Add the mushrooms to the mixture remaining in the medium bowl, tossing to coat. Let stand at room temperature for 10 minutes.

2. Meanwhile, preheat the grill. Thread the mushrooms on double skewers (see tip) and thread the onion wedges on single skewers. Spray the rack—off the grill—with nonstick cooking spray. Place the skewers and bell pepper halves on the rack, cover, and grill at medium, or 6 inches from the heat, turning once, for 6 to 8 minutes, or until just tender. When cool enough to handle, cut the peppers into ¾-inch squares.

3. Place the bread on the rack and grill for 3 to 4 minutes, turning several times, until golden. Rub the toast with the cut garlic and then cut the bread into ½-inch-wide strips Add the apple juice, oil, hot pepper sauce, and salt to the reserved vinegar mixture in the large bowl. Add the mushrooms, onion, and bell peppers. Divide the garlic toasts among 4 plates, top with the mushroom mixture, sprinkle the cheese over, and serve warm or at room temperature.

Helpful hint: Portobello mushrooms have dark-brown caps that measure up to six inches across. They're sold loose at greengrocers and gourmet shops, and in packages at many supermarkets.

FAT: 7G/27%
CALORIES: 235
SATURATED FAT: 2.5G
CARBOHYDRATE: 33G
PROTEIN: 9G
CHOLESTEROL: 11MG
SODIUM: 580MG

TIP

To make it easier to turn the mushroom slices on the grill, thread them onto two skewers instead of just one. Hold both skewers in your hand, keeping the skewers parallel, as you thread the mushrooms on.

CHINESE BARBECUED PORK SALAD

SERVES: 4
WORKING TIME: 40 MINUTES
TOTAL TIME: 50 MINUTES

Based
on a traditional
Szechuan dish, this
salad brings together
pork, pasta, vegetables,
and the surprise of
grilled plums.

¼ cup plum jam

¼ cup reduced-sodium soy
sauce

1 tablespoon grated fresh ginger

2 cloves garlic, minced

¼ teaspoon ground allspice

¾ pound well-trimmed pork
tenderloin

8 ounces capellini pasta, broken
in half

½ pound sugar snap peas,
strings removed

2 purple plums, halved and
pitted

4 scallions

1 cup cherry tomatoes, halved

2 tablespoons fresh lime juice

1 tablespoon dark Oriental
sesame oil

1 tablespoon sesame seeds,
toasted

1. In a large bowl, combine the jam, soy sauce, ginger, garlic, and allspice. Remove 2 tablespoons and use to coat the pork. Let the pork stand at room temperature for 10 minutes. Add ¼ cup of the water to the bowl of dressing and set aside.

2. Meanwhile, in a large pot of boiling water, cook the pasta until just tender. Add the sugar snap peas for the last 2 minutes of cooking time. Drain and rinse under cold water.

3. Preheat the grill. Spray the rack—off the grill—with nonstick cooking spray. Place the pork on the rack, cover, and grill at medium, or 6 inches from the heat, turning once, for 10 minutes, or until the pork is cooked through but still juicy. Meanwhile, grill the plums and scallions, turning once, for 5 minutes, or until slightly charred.

4. When the pork is cool enough to handle, cut it into ¼-by-2-inch strips and add them to the dressing in the bowl. Dice the plums and cut the scallions into ½-inch pieces and add to the bowl. Add the pasta, sugar snap peas, tomatoes, lime juice, and sesame oil, tossing to coat. Divide the salad among 4 plates, top with the sesame seeds, and serve.

Helpful hint: Toast the sesame seeds in a dry skillet over medium heat: Cook, stirring, for 2 to 3 minutes, until the seeds are golden brown.

FAT: 10G/18%
CALORIES: 496
SATURATED FAT: 2.2G
CARBOHYDRATE: 72G
PROTEIN: 31G
CHOLESTEROL: 60MG
SODIUM: 718MG

TANDOORI CHICKEN SALAD

SERVES: 4
WORKING TIME: 20 MINUTES
TOTAL TIME: 40 MINUTES

1 cup plain low-fat yogurt

2 tablespoons fresh lime juice

2 scallions, cut into large pieces

2 teaspoons grated fresh ginger

2 tablespoons mango chutney

1 teaspoon ground cumin

1 teaspoon curry powder

¾ teaspoon salt

¾ pound skinless, boneless chicken breasts, lightly pounded

15-ounce can chick-peas, rinsed and drained

1 small Red Delicious apple, cored and cut into ¾-inch cubes

⅓ cup golden raisins

3 cups mixed greens

3 tablespoons chopped pistachios or cashews

2 cups sliced tomatoes

1. In a food processor or blender, combine the yogurt, lime juice, scallions, ginger, mango chutney, cumin, curry powder, and salt and process to a smooth purée. Transfer ¾ cup of the mixture to a large bowl and set aside. Place the remaining mixture in a medium bowl, add the chicken, turning to coat. Let stand at room temperature for 15 minutes, turning occasionally.

2. Preheat the grill. Spray the rack—off the grill—with nonstick cooking spray. Place the chicken on the rack, cover, and grill at medium, or 6 inches from the heat, turning once, for 8 to 10 minutes, or until cooked through. When cool enough to handle, cut the chicken into 1-inch pieces.

3. Add the chicken to the dressing along with the chick-peas, apple, and raisins, tossing to coat. Divide the greens among 4 plates, spoon the chicken mixture over, and sprinkle with the pistachios. Arrange the tomato slices alongside the chicken and serve warm or at room temperature.

Helpful hints: You can marinate the chicken for up to 8 hours; if you let it stand longer than 30 minutes, cover the bowl and refrigerate it. Green leaf and/or iceberg lettuce are good choices for this salad.

FAT: 7G/18%
CALORIES: 358
SATURATED FAT: 1.4G
CARBOHYDRATE: 45G
PROTEIN: 30G
CHOLESTEROL: 53MG
SODIUM: 725MG

The barbecue grill makes a fine replacement for the white-hot coals in an Indian tandoor (clay oven).

Beef Fajita Salad

Serves: 4
Working time: 20 minutes
Total time: 35 minutes

Classic fajitas are strips of skirt steak (and, usually, onions and peppers) that are marinated, grilled, and served in tortilla wrappers. Our adaptation is a hearty main-dish salad in which chili-rubbed steak, onion, and sliced zucchini are grilled and then combined with corn kernels, cubes of velvety avocado, and fresh cilantro.

¾ cup mild or medium-hot prepared salsa

2 tablespoons fresh lime juice

2 teaspoons chili powder

¾ teaspoon ground cumin

½ teaspoon sugar

½ teaspoon salt

¾ pound well-trimmed sirloin steak

2 zucchini, cut lengthwise into ¾-inch-thick slices

1 red onion, cut crosswise into 4 thick slices

1½ cups frozen corn kernels, thawed

½ avocado, cut into ¾-inch cubes

¼ cup fresh cilantro leaves or shredded basil leaves

4 cups low-fat baked tortilla chips

1. In a large bowl, combine the salsa, lime juice, 1 teaspoon of the chili powder, ½ teaspoon of the cumin, the sugar, and salt and set aside. Rub the steak with the remaining 1 teaspoon chili powder and remaining ¼ teaspoon cumin.

2. Preheat the grill. Spray the rack—off the grill—with nonstick cooking spray. Place the steak, zucchini, and onion on the grill rack. Cover and grill at medium, or 6 inches from the heat, turning once, for 10 to 12 minutes, or until the vegetables are crisp-tender and the steak is medium rare.

3. Place the steak on a plate and let it stand for 10 minutes. Thinly slice it on the diagonal, then cut the slices in half lengthwise, reserving any juices on the plate. Add the beef and juices to the salsa mixture in the bowl. When cool enough to handle, cut the zucchini crosswise into ½-inch-wide strips and coarsely chop the onion. Add the zucchini, onion, corn, avocado, and cilantro to the bowl, tossing to combine. Divide the salad among 4 plates, garnish with the tortilla chips, and serve warm or at room temperature.

Helpful hint: If low-fat baked tortilla chips are not available, substitute oven-baked tortilla triangles: Stack 4 corn tortillas and cut them into 8 wedges. Place the wedges in a single layer on a baking sheet and bake at 400° for about 8 minutes, or until crisp.

Fat: 12g/24%
Calories: 451
Saturated Fat: 2.5g
Carbohydrate: 61g
Protein: 29g
Cholesterol: 57mg
Sodium: 551mg

In
Italy, roast pork loin is
often anointed with
olive oil and sprinkled
with rosemary or
fennel. Here we've used
both of these distinctive
seasonings on grilled
pork tenderloin.
Tomatoes, mushrooms,
and watercress are the
other components
of the salad, which
is served with
grilled "croutons" and
Parmesan curls.

Italian Pork Parmesan Salad

SERVES: 4
WORKING TIME: 20 MINUTES
TOTAL TIME: 30 MINUTES

3 cloves garlic, minced

1½ teaspoons dried rosemary, crumbled

1 teaspoon fennel seeds, crushed

1 teaspoon salt

½ teaspoon freshly ground black pepper

¾ pound well-trimmed pork tenderloin, halved lengthwise

⅓ cup apple juice

2 tablespoons fresh lemon juice

2 teaspoons olive oil

6 ounces French bread, cut into 8 slices

2 tomatoes, cut into thin wedges

2 cups sliced mushrooms

2 cups packed watercress, tough stems removed, chopped

¼ cup shaved Parmesan cheese (see tip)

1. In a medium bowl, combine the garlic, rosemary, fennel, ¼ teaspoon of the salt, and the pepper. Use 2 teaspoons of the mixture to rub over the pork. Add the apple juice, lemon juice, oil, and the remaining ¾ teaspoon salt to the mixture remaining in the bowl; set the dressing aside.

2. Preheat the grill. Spray the rack—off the grill—with nonstick cooking spray. Place the pork on the rack, cover, and grill at medium, or 6 inches from the heat, turning once, for 10 minutes, or until the pork is cooked through but still juicy. Place the bread on the grill for the last 2 to 4 minutes of cooking time, or until toasted on both sides. Place the pork on a plate and let it stand for 10 minutes. Cut the pork into ½-inch-thick slices, reserving any juices on the plate.

3. Add the pork and juices, tomatoes, mushrooms, and watercress to the dressing, tossing to coat. Divide the pork salad and bread among 4 plates, top with the Parmesan, and serve warm or at room temperature.

Helpful hint: If you have a cutting board with a channel or lip to collect the juices, you can transfer the pork to your cutting board, rather than to a plate, to let it stand for 10 minutes before slicing.

TIP

A swivel-bladed vegetable peeler is the perfect tool for cutting broad shavings from a wedge of Parmesan.

FAT: 10G/27%
CALORIES: 328
SATURATED FAT: 3.2G
CARBOHYDRATE: 32G
PROTEIN: 28G
CHOLESTEROL: 65MG
SODIUM: 987MG

BEEF AND ROASTED PEPPER SALAD

SERVES: 4
WORKING TIME: 25 MINUTES
TOTAL TIME: 50 MINUTES

If there are folks in your family who turn up their noses at salad, try serving them this sirloin-and-vegetable platter. Although it's undeniably healthy fare, it's hardly a "diet" dish. Rather, it's a serious main course of grilled steak, corn, and bell peppers. We use fresh corn on the cob for superb summery flavor.

¾ teaspoon chili powder
¾ teaspoon paprika
¾ teaspoon dried thyme
1 teaspoon salt
¼ teaspoon freshly ground black pepper
¾ cup spicy tomato-vegetable juice
1 tablespoon fresh lime juice
1 tablespoon olive oil
1½ teaspoons sugar
¾ pound well-trimmed sirloin steak
4 green bell peppers, seeded and halved lengthwise
1 red onion, cut crosswise into 1-inch-thick slices
4 ears of corn, husks removed
½ cup fresh cilantro leaves
4 cups mixed torn greens

1. In a small bowl, combine the chili powder, paprika, thyme, ¾ teaspoon of the salt, and the black pepper. Measure out ¾ teaspoon of the mixture and place it in a large bowl along with the tomato-vegetable juice, lime juice, oil, sugar, and the remaining ¼ teaspoon salt; whisk to combine and set the dressing aside. Rub the remaining mixture on both sides of the steak and let stand at room temperature for 15 minutes.

2. Meanwhile, preheat the grill. Spray the rack—off the grill—with nonstick cooking spray. Place the steak, bell pepper halves, onion, and corn on the grill rack; cover and grill at medium, or 6 inches from the heat, turning once, for 10 to 12 minutes, or until the vegetables are tender and the meat is medium-rare.

3. Place the steak on a plate and let it stand for 10 minutes. Thinly slice the steak on the diagonal, reserving any juices on the plate. When the vegetables are cool enough to handle, cut the peppers into strips, dice the onion, and cut the kernels off the corn cobs. Add the vegetables and the beef juices to the dressing in the bowl. Add the cilantro and toss to combine. Place the greens on a platter, top with the vegetables and steak, and serve warm or at room temperature.

Helpful hint: You can leave the cilantro out, if you like.

FAT: 10G/29%
CALORIES: 300
SATURATED FAT: 2.4G
CARBOHYDRATE: 33G
PROTEIN: 25G
CHOLESTEROL: 57MG
SODIUM: 754MG

A *smooth, zesty dressing made with sour cream, mustard, lemon juice, garlic, and dried herbs unifies this lovely salad. The reds and golds of the salad are particularly pretty arranged on a bed of emerald-green watercress. In addition to its aesthetic value, the small-leaved salad green is an excellent source of vitamin C.*

GRILLED LEMON CHICKEN SALAD

SERVES: 4
WORKING TIME: 20 MINUTES
TOTAL TIME: 30 MINUTES

1 pound red potatoes, diced

¼ cup fresh lemon juice

3 cloves garlic, minced

1 teaspoon dried oregano

1 teaspoon dried rosemary,
crumbled

¼ teaspoon freshly ground black
pepper

⅓ cup reduced-fat sour cream

2 teaspoons Dijon mustard

½ teaspoon salt

¾ pound skinless, boneless
chicken breasts, lightly pounded
(see tip)

1 pound yellow summer squash,
quartered lengthwise

2 cups small cherry tomatoes,
halved if large

2 cups watercress, tough stems
removed

1. In a medium pot of boiling water, cook the potatoes until firm-tender, about 8 minutes. Drain well.

2. Meanwhile, in a medium bowl, combine the lemon juice, garlic, oregano, rosemary, and pepper. Transfer 2 tablespoons of the mixture to a large bowl and add the sour cream, mustard, and salt; set the dressing aside. Add the chicken to the lemon juice mixture remaining in the medium bowl, tossing to coat. Let stand at room temperature for 10 minutes.

3. Preheat the grill. Spray the rack—off the grill—with nonstick cooking spray. Place the chicken and squash on the grill rack, cover, and grill at medium, or 6 inches from the heat, turning once, for 10 to 12 minutes, or until the chicken is cooked through and the squash is tender. When cool enough to handle, cut the chicken and squash crosswise into ½-inch pieces.

4. Add the potatoes, chicken, squash, and cherry tomatoes to the dressing, tossing to coat. Divide the watercress among 4 plates, top with the chicken mixture, and serve warm or at room temperature.

Helpful hint: Watercress brings a lively tartness to this salad, but you can use a milder green, such as Bibb or Boston lettuce, if you prefer.

FAT: 4G/14%
CALORIES: 264
SATURATED FAT: 1.7G
CARBOHYDRATE: 31G
PROTEIN: 25G
CHOLESTEROL: 56MG
SODIUM: 423MG

TIP

A boneless chicken breast half is naturally thicker at one end. To even it out a bit, place the chicken breast between two sheets of plastic wrap or waxed paper. Pound the thicker part lightly with the flat side of a meat pounder or small skillet.

GRILLED SICILIAN-STYLE SHRIMP SALAD

SERVES: 4
WORKING TIME: 25 MINUTES
TOTAL TIME: 40 MINUTES

¾ pound medium shrimp, shelled and deveined

¼ cup fresh lemon juice

1 tablespoon olive oil

2 cloves garlic, minced

1 teaspoon dried oregano

1 teaspoon fennel seeds, crushed

2 yellow summer squash or zucchini, halved lengthwise

8 plum tomatoes, halved lengthwise

¼ cup reduced-sodium chicken broth, defatted

¼ cup chopped scallions

¼ cup chopped fresh basil

½ teaspoon salt

½ teaspoon grated lemon zest

¼ teaspoon freshly ground black pepper

1 cup diced celery

6 cups mesclun or mixed torn greens

1. Place the shrimp in a medium bowl. In a small bowl, combine the lemon juice, olive oil, garlic, oregano, and fennel. Measure out 2 tablespoons of the lemon juice mixture and toss with the shrimp. Set the shrimp aside at room temperature for 15 minutes.

2. Preheat the grill (with a grill topper, if possible). Spray the rack (or grill topper)—off the grill—with nonstick cooking spray. Place the squash on the grill, brush with some of the lemon juice mixture, cover, and grill at medium, or 6 inches from the heat, turning once, for 4 minutes. Add the shrimp and tomatoes (skin-sides down), brush with any remaining lemon juice mixture, and grill, turning the shrimp once, for 5 to 6 minutes, or until the shrimp are just opaque and the tomato skins are beginning to blister.

3. Meanwhile, in a large bowl, combine the broth, scallions, basil, salt, lemon zest, and pepper. Cut the squash into bite-size chunks and dice the tomatoes. Add the squash and tomatoes to the dressing along with the shrimp and celery, tossing to coat. Divide the greens among 4 plates, spoon the salad over, and serve warm or at room temperature.

Helpful hint: We leave the tails on the shrimp for a prettier presentation, but if you prefer, you can remove the tails when shelling the shrimp.

FAT: 5G/27%
CALORIES: 167
SATURATED FAT: 0.8G
CARBOHYDRATE: 14G
PROTEIN: 18G
CHOLESTEROL: 105MG
SODIUM: 459MG

The heat of the grill concentrates the flavor of the tomatoes here, and adds delicious depth to this lavish salad. The ingredients offer a study in contrasts, with pungent garlic playing off against tart lemon juice, sizzling shrimp against cool greens, and "melting" tomatoes against crisp celery. A basket of grilled garlic bread is the perfect partner for this dish.

GRILLED CHICKEN AND THREE-PEPPER SALAD

SERVES: 4
WORKING TIME: 20 MINUTES
TOTAL TIME: 45 MINUTES

*C*hicken kebabs marinated in a Middle-Eastern-style minty yogurt sauce go straight from skewer to salad bowl here, along with grilled onion and a bright trio of bell peppers. It's a salad that's best (and most sensibly) made when local bell peppers are available in all the glory of their rich hues—and when they're far cheaper than out-of-season imported peppers.

1 cup plain low-fat yogurt

¼ cup chopped fresh mint

2 cloves garlic, minced

1 tablespoon fresh lemon juice

1 teaspoon dried oregano

⅛ teaspoon ground allspice

¾ pound skinless, boneless chicken breasts, cut crosswise into 1-inch-wide strips

1 red onion, cut into thin wedges

3 bell peppers, mixed colors, seeded and halved lengthwise

½ teaspoon sugar

½ teaspoon salt

⅛ teaspoon freshly ground black pepper

2 cups seeded, diced cucumber

2 cups mesclun or mixed torn greens

1. In a medium bowl, combine the yogurt, mint, garlic, lemon juice, oregano, and allspice. Transfer ¾ cup of the mixture to a large bowl and set aside. Add the chicken to the mixture remaining in the medium bowl, tossing to coat. Let stand at room temperature for 15 minutes.

2. Meanwhile, preheat the grill. Thread the chicken and onion wedges onto separate skewers. Spray the rack—off the grill—with nonstick cooking spray. Place the onion skewers and bell pepper halves on the rack. Cover and grill at medium, or 6 inches from the heat, turning once, for 3 minutes. Add the chicken skewers and grill, turning once, for 12 minutes, or until the chicken is cooked through and the vegetables are tender.

3. Stir the sugar, salt, and black pepper into the yogurt mixture in the large bowl. Add the cucumber, grilled chicken, and onion, tossing to coat. Cut the bell peppers into strips and add to the bowl. Divide the mesclun among 4 plates, top with the chicken mixture, and serve warm or at room temperature.

Helpful hint: If there's any yogurt mixture remaining in the bowl after the chicken has marinated, discard it: Don't add it to the yogurt mixture in the large bowl. The marinade, having come in contact with raw poultry, poses the risk of salmonella poisoning.

FAT: 2G/10%
CALORIES: 180
SATURATED FAT: 0.9G
CARBOHYDRATE: 16G
PROTEIN: 25G
CHOLESTEROL: 53MG
SODIUM: 379MG

GLOSSARY

Arugula—A peppery Italian salad green; also called rocket or roquette. Arugula's elongated dark-green leaves look something like dandelion leaves, but they're rounded rather than sharply toothed. This assertive green has a slightly hot, slightly bitter flavor that adds punch to salads; it can also be sautéed and served as a vegetable. Choose a crisp bunch of arugula that isn't yellowed; store it in the refrigerator for no longer than a day or two. After untying the bunch, trim the stems and wash the leaves carefully, as you would spinach.

Balsamic vinegar—A dark red vinegar made from the unfermented juice of pressed grapes, most commonly the white Trebbiano, and aged in wooden casks. The authentic version is produced in a small region in Northern Italy, around Modena, and tastes richly sweet with a slight sour edge. Because this vinegar is so mild, you can make dressings and marinades with less oil.

Basil—A highly fragrant herb with a flavor somewhere between licorice and cloves. Fresh basil, widely available in summer, is a must for Italian-style salads; dried basil is quite flavorful and is a fine seasoning for dressings. Store fresh basil by placing the stems in a container of water and covering the leaves loosely with a plastic bag.

Broccoli—A deep-green vegetable that consists of a cloud of buds atop thick, fleshy stalks. One of the most nutritious vegetables you can eat, broccoli originated in Italy. When young and fresh, broccoli is tender and delicately sweet (old broccoli is tough and has a strong cabbagy flavor and odor). Choose bright green broccoli—a touch of blue or purple is fine—with tightly closed buds and crisp, firm stalks. If a recipe calls for broccoli florets, cut off the stems about 1 inch below the buds and separate into small sprigs. (Don't discard the stalks; save them for another use, such as soup-making.)

Buttermilk—A milk product made by adding a special bacterial culture to nonfat or low-fat milk. Thick and tangy, with a rich flavor despite its low fat content, buttermilk is a wonderful base for salad dressings. Use within 1 week of purchase.

Cabbage—A compact-headed vegetable with crisp, sturdy leaves. Not just for slaw, green and red cabbage (as well as Savoy, a crinkly-leaved variety) are versatile salad ingredients. Cabbage is available all year round, with Savoy more abundant during the autumn and winter. Select a head that feels heavy for its size; the outer leaves should be free of blemishes. Different types of cabbage can almost always be used interchangeably.

Cayenne pepper—A hot spice ground from dried red chili peppers. Add cayenne to taste when preparing Mexican, Tex-Mex, Indian, Chinese, and Caribbean dishes; start with just a small amount, as cayenne is fiery-hot.

Celery—A vegetable that takes the form of a long, narrow bunch of pale-green stalks with leafy tops. Crunchy and refreshing, celery is delicious raw, as a component of a salad or crudité platter. Choose a crisp, firm bunch of celery with fresh-looking leaves; store it in a plastic bag in the refrigerator. Celery will keep for up to two weeks.

Cilantro/Coriander—A lacy-leaved green herb (called by both names). The plant's seeds are dried and used as a spice (known as coriander). The fresh herb, much used in Mexican and Asian cuisines, looks like pale flat-leaf parsley and is strongly aromatic. Store fresh cilantro by placing the stems in a container of water and covering the leaves loosely with a plastic bag. Coriander seeds are important in Mexican and Indian cuisines; sold whole or ground, they have a somewhat citrusy flavor that complements both sweet and savory dishes.

Cumin—A pungent, peppery-tasting spice essential to many Middle Eastern, Asian, Mexican, and Mediterranean dishes. Available ground or as whole seeds; the spice can be toasted in a dry skillet to bring out its flavor.

Garlic—The edible bulb of a plant closely related to onions, leeks, and chives. Garlic can be pungently assertive or sweetly mild, depending on how it is prepared: Minced or crushed garlic yields a more powerful flavor than whole or halved cloves. Whereas sautéing turns garlic rich and savory, slow simmering or roasting produces a mild, mellow flavor. Select firm, plump heads with dry skins; avoid heads that have begun to sprout. Store garlic in an open or loosely covered container in a cool, dark place for up to 2 months.

Ginger, fresh—A thin-skinned root used as a seasoning. Fresh ginger adds sweet pungency to Asian and Indian dishes. Tightly wrapped, unpeeled fresh ginger can be refrigerated for 1 week or frozen for up to 6 months. Ground ginger is not a true substitute for fresh, but it will lend a warming flavor to foods.

Honey—A liquid sweetener made by honeybees from flower nectar. It ranges in flavor from mild (orange blossom) to very strong (buckwheat). Deliciously versatile, honey adds a nicely rounded sweetness to savory dressings and sauces. Store honey at room temperature. If it crystallizes, place the open jar in a pan of warm water for a few minutes; or microwave it for 10 to 15 seconds, or until the honey liquifies.

Juice, citrus—The flavorful liquid component of oranges, lemon, limes, tangerines, and the like. Freshly squeezed citrus juice has an inimitable freshness that livens up low-fat foods. Frozen juice concentrates make a tangy base for sweet or savory dressings. An inexpensive hand reamer makes quick work of juicing citrus fruits.

Lettuce, Bibb—A butterhead lettuce that forms a small, cup-shaped head of grass-green leaves. As the term "butterhead" suggests, Bibb lettuce leaves are soft and delicate, with a sweet, mild flavor. Use this lettuce when other salad ingredients and the dressing are not too strong-flavored or acidic.

Lettuce, Boston—A butterhead lettuce with pale yellowish-green leaves that form a medium-sized head shaped like a rose. Boston lettuce is a bit sturdier than Bibb (above), but the same serving suggestions apply.

Lettuce, iceberg—A compact, cabbage-shaped crisphead lettuce with a very mild flavor. Although its taste is unexciting, iceberg lettuce is uniquely crisp and crunchy. Chunks or shreds of iceberg go well with hot or spicy ingredients: This lettuce is often used in taco salads and other Mexican or Tex-Mex dishes.

Lettuce, red or green leaf—Two types of lettuces that grow in loose, open bunches, rather than forming tight heads. Leaf letuces, fresh-tasting but not assertive in flavor, are versatile salad ingredients. The dark bronze color of the red-leaf type makes a handsome addition to an otherwise all-green salad bowl.

Lettuce, romaine—A sturdy lettuce whose leaves form an oblong, fairly loose head. Romaine (also called cos) has a distinctively sweet taste; its leaves are pale at the base, shading to a deep green at the tips. Romaine is the lettuce tradition-ally used for Caesar salad; it resists wilting and holds up well under acidic or warm dressings.

Mesclun—A mixture of baby lettuce leaves and other greens, fresh herbs, and, sometimes, edible flowers. Mesclun (pronounced MES-klen) is a Provençal word that means "mixture." When buying mesclun, which is sold both loose and packaged, check to be sure you're getting tiny, tender leaves, and not mature lettuce torn into small pieces; there should be a number of different greens for a pleasing variety of taste and texture. The mixture should smell fresh; a sickly-sweet aroma signals decay.

Mint—A large family of herbs used to impart a refreshingly heady fragrance and cool aftertaste to foods; the most common types are spearmint and peppermint. As with other fresh herbs, mint is best added toward the end of the cooking time. Dried mint is fairly intense, so a pinch goes a long way. Store fresh mint the same way as fresh cilantro.

Olive oil—A fragrant oil pressed from olives. Olive oil, one of the signature ingredients of Italian cuisine, is the ingredient of choice for vinaigrettes and other dressings when vegetable oil is called for. Olive oil comes in different grades, reflecting the method used to refine the oil and the resulting level of acidity. The finest, most expensive oil is cold-pressed extra-virgin, which is the best choice for salad dressings and other uncooked (or lightly cooked) foods. "Virgin" and "pure" olive oils are slightly more acidic with less olive flavor, and are fine for most types of cooking.

Onion, red—Medium- to large-sized spherical onions with purplish-red skins. Red onions are somewhat milder than yellow or white globe onions; they don't require cooking to mellow their flavor, so they're perfect for salads. Bermuda onions or Spanish onions can be substituted for red onions.

Parmesan cheese—An intensely flavored, hard grating cheese. Genuine Italian Parmesan, stamped "Parmigiano-Reggiano" on the rind, is produced in the Emilia-Romagna region, and tastes richly nutty with a slight sweetness. Buy Parmesan in blocks and grate it as needed for best flavor and freshness. For a fine, fluffy texture that melts into hot foods, grate the cheese in a hand-cranked grater.

Radishes—Small root vegetables with crisp, juicy flesh and a slightly peppery flavor. The radishes most commonly used in salads are spherical or oval, with red skins and white flesh; white "icicle" radishes that resemble small carrots are also popular. Choose firm radishes with bright green leaves; refrigerate them in a plastic bag and use within five days of purchase.

Rice, long-grain—A type of rice with grains much longer than they are wide. Long-grain rice remains fluffy and separate when cooked and is excellent for salads. Converted rice, which has been specially processed to preserve nutrients, takes slightly longer to cook than regular white rice. Rice is an ideal starting point for hearty, healthful salads because it is filling, very low in fat, and absorbs flavors beautifully.

Scallions—Immature onions (also called green onions) with a mild and slightly sweet flavor. Both the white bulb and the green tops can be used in salads; the green tops, cut into sections, sliced, or chopped, make an attractive garnish. To prepare, trim off the base of the bulb or root end and any blemished ends of the green tops. Remove the outermost, thin skin around the bulb. Cut the white portion from the green tops and use separately, or use together in the same dish.

Sesame oil, Oriental—A dark, polyunsaturated oil pressed from toasted sesame seeds, that is used as a flavor enhancer in many Asian and Indian dishes. Do not confuse the Oriental oil with its lighter colored counterpart, which is cold-pressed from untoasted sesame seeds and imparts a much milder flavor. Store either version in the refrigerator for up to 6 months.

Sour cream—A soured dairy product, made by treating sweet cream with a lactic acid culture. Regular sour cream contains at least 18 percent milk fat by volume; reduced-fat sour cream contains 4 percent fat; nonfat sour cream is, of course, fat-free. Sour cream is a healthier substitute for heavy cream or mayonnaise in salad dressings; both the reduced-fat and nonfat versions can be substituted for regular sour cream in such recipes. Nonfat sour cream does behave differently when heated, and to avoid curdling, do not subject any type of sour cream to high heat.

Soy sauce, reduced-sodium—A condiment made from fermented soybeans, wheat, and salt used to add a salty, slightly sweet flavor to food. Soy sauce is especially at home in stir-fries and Asian-style salads. Keep in mind that reduced-sodium sauces add the same flavor but much less sodium.

Spinach, fresh—A nutrient-rich, dark-green, leafy vegetable. Fresh spinach has crisp, emerald green leaves; it will keep its bright color if not overcooked. When buying fresh spinach, choose springy, green bunches; avoid withered or yellowing leaves. Wash spinach carefully, as it is often gritty: Submerge the leaves in a large bowl of lukewarm water, swirl them with your hands, then lift out the leaves. Even bagged spinach labeled "prewashed" should be rinsed.

Sugar snap peas—A type of sweet peas with edible pods. Developed in the 1970s, sugar snaps are a cross between regular peas and snow peas. Unlike snow peas, which are flat, sugar snaps are plump, with fully formed peas inside the pods. Before eating sugar snaps, pinch off the tips and remove the string that runs along both the front and back of the pod. Eat sugar snaps raw, or steam or blanch them very briefly.

Sweet potato—A starchy tuber with sweet yellow or orange flesh, sometimes mistakenly called a yam. As a change from white potatoes in salads, sweet potatoes contribute a distinctive nutty-sweet flavor and vivid orange color. They also offer vitamin C and a good deal of beta carotene. Choose smooth-skinned potatoes with tapered ends and no blemishes. Store sweet potatoes in a cool, dark place (not in the refrigerator) for up to 1 month; they'll stay fresh for a week at room temperature.

Tarragon—A potent, sweet herb with a licorice- or anise-like taste; often used with chicken or fish. Dried tarragon loses its flavor quickly; check its potency by crushing a little between your fingers and sniffing for the strong aroma. As with most herbs, you may substitute 1 teaspoon dried for each tablespoon of fresh.

Thyme—A lemony-tasting member of the mint family frequently paired with bay leaves in Mediterranean-style dishes and rice-based preparations. The dried herb, both ground and leaf, is an excellent substitute for the fresh.

Vinegar, red and white wine—Vinegars made by fermenting red or white wine. Use these vinegars in vinaigrettes and other dressings, especially those that employ Italian or French flavors. (Use red wine vinegar with assertive ingredients, white wine vinegar in more delicate salads.) For a change, try champagne or sherry vinegar, or a wine vinegar flavored with herbs.

Vinegar, rice—A pale vinegar made from fermented rice, it is milder than most other types of vinegar. Rice vinegar's light, clean flavor, much favored in Asian cooking, allows you to make dressing with less oil. Japanese rice vinegar is widely available; be sure to buy the unseasoned type.

Watercress—A slightly peppery-tasting aquatic herb that adds zip to salads and cooked dishes. The assertive flavor of watercress provides a peppery counterpoint to savory or sweet flavors. To prepare, rinse the bunch of watercress under cold water and blot dry with paper towels. Remove the tough stalks and use just the tender stems, or, for a more delicate flavor, use only the leaves.

Yogurt, low-fat and nonfat—Delicately tart cultured milk products made from low-fat or skim milk. Plain yogurt makes a healthful base for dressings—a more healthful substitute for mayonnaise or cream.

Zest, citrus—The thin, outermost colored part of the rind of citrus fruits that contains strongly flavored oils. Zest imparts an intense flavor that makes a refreshing contrast to the richness of meat, poultry, or fish. Remove the zest with a grater, citrus zester, or vegetable peeler; be careful to remove only the colored layer, not the bitter white pith beneath it.

Index

TIME LIFE BOOKS

Time-Life Books is a division of Time Life Inc.

TIME LIFE INC.

PRESIDENT and CEO: George Artandi

TIME-LIFE BOOKS

PRESIDENT: John D. Hall
PUBLISHER/MANAGING EDITOR: Neil Kagan

GREAT TASTE~LOW FAT
Main-Dish Salads

DEPUTY EDITOR: Marion Ferguson Briggs
MARKETING DIRECTOR: Cheryl D. Eklind

Consulting Editor: Catherine Boland Hackett

Vice President, Director of Finance: Christopher Hearing
Vice President, Book Production: Marjann Caldwell
Director of Operations: Eileen Bradley
Director of Photography and Research: John Conrad Weiser
Director of Editorial Administration (Acting): Barbara Levitt
Production Manager: Marlene Zack
Quality Assurance Manager: James King
Library: Louise D. Forstall

Design for Great Taste~Low Fat by David Fridberg of
Miles Fridberg Molinaroli, Inc.

REBUS, INC.

PUBLISHER: Rodney M. Friedman
EDITORIAL DIRECTOR: Charles L. Mee

Editorial Staff for *Main-Dish Salads*
Director, Recipe Development and Photography: Grace Young
Editorial Director: Kate Slate
Senior Recipe Developer: Sandra Rose Gluck
Recipe Developers: Helen Jones, Paul Piccuito
Writer: Bonnie J. Slotnick
Managing Editor: Julee Binder Shapiro
Editorial Assistant: James W. Brown, Jr.
Nutritionists: Hill Nutrition Associates

Art Director: Timothy Jeffs
Photographer: Lisa Koenig
Photographer's Assistants: Alix Berenberg, Katie Bleacher Everard,
    Rainer Fehringer, Petra Liebetanz
Food Stylists: Catherine Paukner, Karen Pickus, Karen Tack
Assistant Food Stylists: Charles Davis, Tracy Donovan, Susan Kadel
Prop Stylist: Debrah Donahue
Prop Coordinator: Karin Martin

Library of Congress Cataloging-in-Publication Data

Main-dish salads.
p.   cm. -- (Great taste, low fat)
Includes index.
ISBN 0-7835-4566-5
1. Salads. 2. Entrées (Cookery) 3. Low-fat diet--Recipes.
I. Time-Life Books. II. Series.
TX740.M227   1997
641.8'3--dc21

96-49782
CIP

METRIC CONVERSION CHARTS

VOLUME EQUIVALENTS
(fluid ounces/milliliters and liters)

US	Metric
1 tsp	5 ml
1 tbsp (½ fl oz)	15 ml
¼ cup (2 fl oz)	60 ml
⅓ cup	80 ml
½ cup (4 fl oz)	120 ml
⅔ cup	160 ml
¾ cup (6 fl oz)	180 ml
1 cup (8 fl oz)	240 ml
1 qt (32 fl oz)	950 ml
1 qt + 3 tbsps	1 L
1 gal (128 fl oz)	4 L

Conversion formula
Fluid ounces X 30 = milliliters
1000 milliliters = 1 liter

WEIGHT EQUIVALENTS
(ounces and pounds/grams and kilograms)

US	Metric
¼ oz	7 g
½ oz	15 g
¾ oz	20 g
1 oz	30 g
8 oz (½ lb)	225 g
12 oz (¾ lb)	340 g
16 oz (1 lb)	455 g
35 oz (2.2 lbs)	1 kg

Conversion formula
Ounces X 28.35 = grams
1000 grams = 1 kilogram

LINEAR EQUIVALENTS
(inches and feet/centimeters and meters)

US	Metric
¼ in	.75 cm
½ in	1.5 cm
¾ in	2 cm
1 in	2.5 cm
6 in	15 cm
12 in (1 ft)	30 cm
39 in	1 m

Conversion formula
Inches X 2.54 = centimeters
100 centimeters = 1 meter

TEMPERATURE EQUIVALENTS
(Fahrenheit/Celsius)

US	Metric
0° (freezer temperature)	-18°
32° (water freezes)	0°
98.6°	37°
180° (water simmers*)	82°
212° (water boils*)	100°
250° (low oven)	120°
350° (moderate oven)	175°
425° (hot oven)	220°
500° (very hot oven)	260°

*at sea level

Conversion formula
Degrees Fahrenheit minus
32 ÷ 1.8 = degrees Celsius